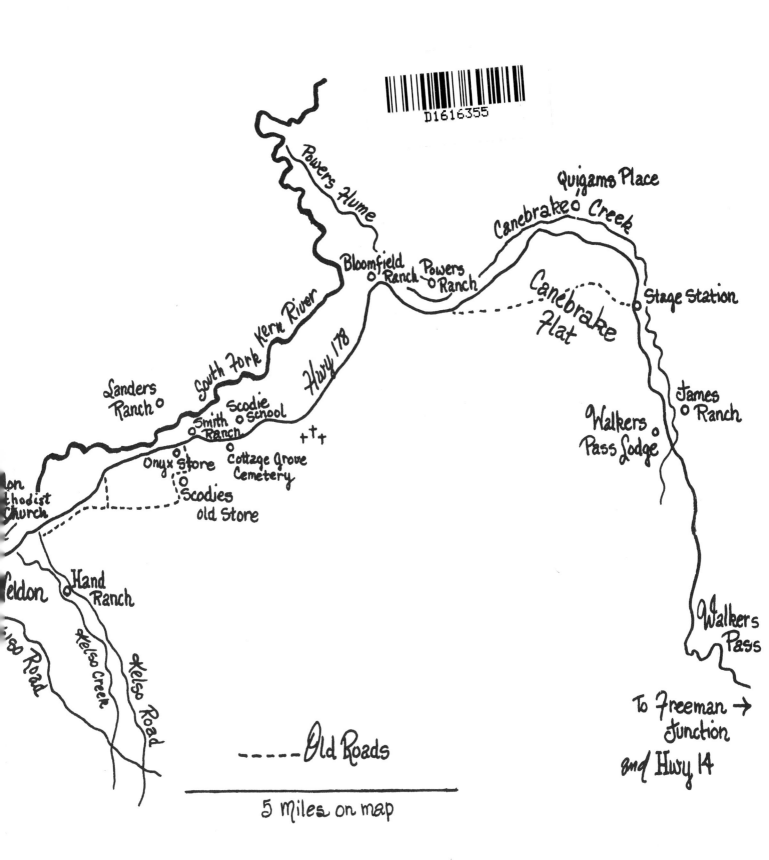

Powers Flume

Quigams Place

Canebrake o Creek

Bloomfield Ranch

Powers Ranch

Canebrake Flat

Stage Station

South Fork Kern River

Hwy 178

Landers Ranch

Scodie School

Smith Ranch

James o Ranch

Walkers Pass Lodge

Onyx Store

Cottage Grove Cemetery

on thodist Church

Scodies old Store

Weldon

Hand Ranch

Walkers Pass

180 Road

Kelso Creek

Kelso Road

To Freeman →
Junction
and Hwy 14

- - - - - Old Roads

5 miles on map

South Fork Country

South Fork Country

by Bob Powers

THE ARTHUR H. CLARK COMPANY
Glendale, California   1988

SECOND PRINTING — MAY 1972
THIRD PRINTING — MAY 1976
FOURTH PRINTING — NOVEMBER 1980
FIFTH PRINTING - 1988

Library of Congress Catalog Card No. 72-180832
ISBN No. 0-87062-188-2

PRINTED IN THE UNITED STATES OF AMERICA BY WESTERNLORE PRESS

Dedicated to my wife, Marjorie, who has been helpful as well as patient through the years of research . . .

Acknowledgments

I WISH to thank my many friends living in and around the Kern River Valley for the countless hours they have given me in my research for this book. I would like also to express my appreciation to the South Forkers who have since passed on, who had a kindred interest in the early history of this mountain valley, especially Ella P. Smith, who had previously gathered much of the material used by me on the Methodist Church at Weldon.

My special thanks to Bob Ettner for his proofreading of the manuscript, and to Jess Stockton and Dr. Harland Boyd for their assistance in tying down dates and places. To Ken Wortley, the former editor of the *Sierra Rainbow*, for the help he has given me in the way of pictures and advice. Also thanks to my good friend Jeanette Rogers for her fine map making, and to Jeff Edwards, of Edwards Studio in Porterville, for his untiring efforts in copying pictures for me.

To John Wofford, Tad Lonergan, and Bill Riffle, for the interest and encouragement that helped me push through to publishing time. To my mother, Isabell Powers, as well as the rest of the family, for the help and consideration they have given me, and to my Dad, the late Marvin P. Powers, for instilling in me the love for the history of these mountain valleys that started me on my research.

This expression of my gratitude to those mentioned above is but a feeble attempt to express my deep appreciation.

BOB POWERS.

Foreword

SOUTH FORK COUNTRY is the account of the settlement and pioneer happenings of the South Fork of the Kern River. This collection of stories was written by the author with the hope that he would be able to preserve for future generations some of the unusual character, the spirit of friendship and cooperation that has prevailed among the residents of this little mountain valley.

Bob Powers, a great-grandson of Thomas H. Smith, who settled on the South Fork in 1861, was born in Old Kernville in 1924. He attended the South Fork Union Grammar School and spent the first thirty years of his life in the South Fork Valley. His early life was closely tied to the family cattle business, and when he was a year old he rode horseback the fifty miles from the ranch headquarters at Onyx to the summer cow camp at Fish Creek—on a pillow in front of his father.

Bob started driving teams in the hay fields when he was just eight years old and saw the change of horsepower to tractor power. He not only worked cattle for most of the ranches in the Valley but also worked in the hay fields of many of the ranches there too.

In 1951 Bob married Marjorie Martin, and to this union were born four boys and one girl. In 1956 he went to work for the U.S. Forest Service in the Sequoia National Forest, where he is presently employed as Recreational Officer in Kernville, California. Some of his jobs include the supervision of work on the same mountain trails which his grandfather, Jim Powers, worked for the Forest Reserve in 1900, and the counting of the cattle each spring into the Forest, where his family has been grazing their cattle for sixty-six years.

The author has intended to convey to the reader something of the sterling qualities of the pioneers, of which consideration for others was characteristic in their daily association with those around them. This was paramount among these old-timers of the South Fork. If this book serves to help keep their memory green, he will feel as though his time has been well spent.

Table of Contents

I ~ The Canebrake

To THE casual weekend traveler the turn-off from Highway 14 onto Highway 178 at Freeman Junction simply indicates the last leg of a trip from Southern California to Lake Isabella and a couple of days of fishing and relaxation. The forty some odd miles pass quickly. There is time enough to look at the scenery after a campsite has been found and the kids fed.

But a more leisurely and imaginative observer soon comes to know that this area, loosely called the South Fork, is rich in local history. They learn that the Valley was once the sole domain of the Tubatulabal Indian until a day in May, 1834, when Captain Joseph R. Walker, who had just spent the winter of 1833-34 in Monterey, became the first Caucasian to work his way up the South Fork on his way to the rendezvous with Lieutenant Bonneville. They also learn that this historic pass echoed the creak of ox yokes and the pop of the whip as pioneer bullwhackers, like Eph Johnson, hauled freight from Visalia over this route to the mines around Lone Pine. And by 1860 white settlers began to stake out claims along this picturesque river where many of their descendants still live.

The view from the car for the first seven miles west from Highway 14 is almost exactly what could be seen from the window of a stage coach, dust permitting. In the 1870's a stage line crossed the Sierras at this spot. As you follow the highway down the western side of Walker's Pass, you are in the upper reaches of the South Fork Valley—so named for the fork of the Kern River which flows into the valley bottom further down the road. The South Fork was originally called the Rio Chiquito, or Little River, by some of the old folks.

All interesting history of the area is not necessarily ancient. For instance, the canyon off to the south after you cross Canebrake Creek was once the site of a still, maintained during Pro-

hibition by an enterprising Valley resident named Victor Hugo. His product was not as enduring as that of his literary namesake, but Hugo's occupation was considered every bit as honorable — provided he did not get caught. Oldtimers tell of Hugo's efforts to out-shuffle Internal Revenue agents. A visit from the Revenuers meant a lapse in production until Hugo could set up shop in another location. This was extremely irritating, inconvenient, and unprofitable. So Hugo would surround his current operation with a network of booby traps consisting of wires strung through the sagebrush at strategic points. From these wires were suspended cow bells, tin cans, and other noise-makers designed to warn the proprietor of the approach of the spoilsport minions of the law. Victor Hugo lived about a mile up Canebrake Creek, where he had an apple orchard and a house with a large attic. The orchard was a sideline. The attic was the last known location of the still.

This creek was named Canebrake in the fall of 1853 by Lieutenant R. S. Williamson when searching for a railroad route over the Sierra Nevada. The Indians he found camped there in the fall of that year were collecting a kind of bulrush or cane. On the leaves of these plants was found a substance very much like sugar.

Walker Pass Lodge, about three miles down the highway from Walker Pass Summit, was built during the 1930's from lumber salvaged from the remains of James Station. A lone rock chimney on a sagebrush flat a half mile north of the Lodge is all that remains of James Station now. At one time it was the garden spot of the South Fork, with a flourishing orchard and truck garden which provided apples and vegetable products to the miners of the desert and Kernville area. The station was built around 1910 by Billy James and his wife, Ava. Billy came to the Valley as a boy in the mid-1870's. He earned his

Rock fireplace marks the spot where James Station once stood.

living by various means over the years. In 1880 he was a laborer at the Big Blue Mine in Kernville. He helped build the primitive roads through the Valley when horsepower referred to real horses. In later years, Billy was a caretaker at the Edison Company intake up the Kern River above Kernville.

Perhaps the thing Billy did that will be longest remembered was to establish James Station. In those days, every family had a kitchen garden to supply produce for the table. Mining camp residents were not agriculturally inclined, however, and lack of refrigeration and difficulty of transportation made fresh fruits and vegetables luxury items to them. This created a sellers market and made the Station a going concern from the start. Billy delivered the garden goods in a covered wagon drawn by four horses, while Ava stayed in her kitchen preparing savory home-cooked meals for hungry, road-weary travelers. The children born to the James family were four boys—Henry, George, William, and Bert, and a girl named Ruth.

Frequent visitors to the South Fork will recognize the big black walnut tree on the left side of the road, four miles down from Walker Pass Lodge. Its cool shade on a summer day seems to invite the traveler to stop and rest, eat a picnic lunch, or simply enjoy a moment of peace and quiet. Many tourists and residents alike

2

stop here, unknowingly continuing a custom that has gone on for one hundred or more years that this tree has been standing. Family records indicate that Thomas Hooper Smith planted the tree and built a stage station on this spot in the 1870's. Operation of the station was turned over to Asa Finley, descendants of whom still live in the Valley. In 1875, when the railroad reached Mojave, this portion of the stage run was discontinued, as the run terminated at Onyx.

Before the road was rebuilt in the 1930's, it turned west from the stage station. Crossing the pass, the road went down through Canebrake Flats in a long, straight sweep to the Bloomfield Ranch. When horseless carriages became the vogue, this stretch of road was the scene of many an early-day drag race at breathtaking speeds of thirty-five to forty miles per hour. Who could resist the temptation to "open her up and see what she'd do" on that long, flat straightaway? So it is not surprising that the old time South

Billie James, taken in the 1880's.

Billie James delivers garden produce to Randsburg in 1914.

Black walnut tree planted by Smith in 1870.

Fork Valley had traffic accidents—some tragic.

A remnant of the old stage station, the flat stone that served as a doorstep, was used by Phil and Myrta Glezen who homesteaded on Canebrake Flat. The Glezens removed the stone from the ruins of the station in 1914 and took it to their home, where it remained as a doorstep for fifty-three years.

A mile below the old stage station was where the old Tubatulabal Indian, known only as Quigam, lived. This old Indian, when a small boy, remembered seeing Joseph Walker come through the Valley in 1834. Below the road and across the creek is the small flat used for so many years as a family garden. Quigam was steeped in the traditional tribal superstitions, and for some unknown reason believed his only daughter was a witch. Mrs. Thomas H. Smith told in later years how the little girl had run a mile up the creek from the tribal rancheria to where the Smiths lived at the Canebrake Station. Although the girl spoke very little English, she made Mrs. Smith understand that her father thought she was a witch and was going to kill her. Putting the child in her own bed, Mrs. Smith met the father and another Indian at the door and gave them such a sound talking to that they never again attempted to take the girl's life.

In the early 1900's a cloudburst brought a wall of water down Canebrake Creek. Quigam and his family, forewarned by the roaring of the approaching disaster, made it to safety on the bank. When the daughter remembered that her smoking tobacco was stashed out in the creek bottom, with the devotion of a true addict, she tried to outrun the flood and retrieve her precious tobacco. But unfortunately her wind wasn't the best, and she lost the race. Her father made a half-hearted attempt to bury her by placing the body in a gully and piling a few rocks over it. A few days later the James children, while walking down the creek, came across the girl's remains, partly eaten by coyotes. After getting help, they put enough rocks on the grave to keep the animals away.

A few years later, while on one of his proverbial drunks, Quigam fell asleep in his little shack on the north bank of the creek. Due either to a dropped smoking pipe or a log rolling out of the open hearth, his dwelling caught fire. In those days there were few who traveled that way, as the road still went over Canebrake Flat.

Left to right, Tubatulabul Indian, Quigam; his squaw; and friend Bill Chico.

3

Picture of Canebrake Flat, taken in 1947.

It was a while before someone came by and reported what had happened. Quigam had burned to death in the fire, and his dogs, after going several days without food, had proceeded to pick his bones.

A few hundred yards down the creek from where Quigam dwelled, lived an old Indian woman known as Iagora, who was famous for her basket making. This entire creek was used as campsites for the early tribes. Grind holes in the large rock above the creek now provide mute evidence of early Indian activities.

Canebrake Flat does not look particularly menacing. It looks flat. The soil is deep and fertile and appears to be an excellent spot to grow crops. Do not be deceived. The Flat has been the scene of many a battle between man and nature due to lack of water. Rain storms sweeping into the Valley from the west drop most of their precious moisture on the Greenhorn Mountains. As they move east to the South Fork they diminish in intensity. Perhaps one year in ten

will bring the Flat enough rain to produce a decent crop. This one tantalizing year is enough to encourage those with an instinct for the land to keep trying. Probably as long as there are farmers, someone will plant Canebrake Flat and hope for a miracle.

John Ripley attempted to make a living off Canebrake Flat during the 1890's. He was one of the first to try and, like the others, he failed. No believer in miracles, Ripley took nature at her word and moved to Caliente. There he established a hotel and freight line, both of which prospered come rain or shine. Many farmers coming to Canebrake after Ripley had reason to wish they had followed his example.

One pioneer, Preston Powers, tried to beat the odds by supplementing sparse rainfall with water from Canebrake Creek. He filed a claim on the water rights early in 1900, and dug a ditch from the creek to his land. The creek proved as temperamental as any other water in the vicinity, and went dry that year. The ditch is

4

still there, carrying water under the road — when there is water.

The year 1945 was a good year for rain on the Canebrake Flat. Marvin Powers, who owned the north side of the Flat, brought in a bumper crop of barley. This freakish turn of events so encouraged one of Powers' sons that, against the advice of his elders, and in spite of his own experience, he leased 360 acres from his father and went to work. He grubbed out sagebrush that had overrun the fields since the acreage had last been planted. He tried to make the house on the place habitable, though it was in far worse shape than the land. At night he was kept awake by domestic cats gone wild. They yowled and tried to claw their way through the gunny sacks nailed over the windows that had been innocent of glass for years.

Young Powers supported his farming venture by working on the Bloomfield Ranch, several miles down the Valley. He rode back and forth on horseback. In the bits and pieces of time left in the day, he managed to clear the land, repair the reservoir, and put in ten acres of alfalfa and sixty acres of barley. He worked hard. As he worked he waited for the bumper crop — his miracle.

What actually happened, while by no means miraculous, was somewhat unusual. For the first time in thirty years Canebrake Creek went dry. The alfalfa was first to go. The six-inch high barley dried up, leaving not even good pasture, much less a crop of grain.

Having established a downhill trend, Powers' fortunes continued in that direction. While trying to ride a black mare on the Smith Ranch— one that had become a challenge to all the young cowboys in the area—he broke his arm. Shortly thereafter his house caught fire. When things reached the point where he was subsisting on a more or less steady diet of jackrabbit, Powers gave it up and moved out. Thus, another Canebrake farmer bit the dust.

The southeast portion of Canebrake Flat is where Phil and Myrta Glezen had their homestead. Phil, a registered pharmacist, was the first one in the Valley, and worked for Lee Rankin at the Onyx Store. Between 1921 and 1933 he operated the store. As was the custom, Phil hung his pharmacist's certificate on the wall behind the counter. Recognizing it as a symbol of a higher degree of education than could be attained at the Weldon School, men who worked on the Onyx Ranch contrived from time to time to keep Phil humble by adorning the certificate with objects of any earthy and ribald nature. Worked too!

Phil never needed a larger hat!

Powers family at Chimney Meadow on their way to the high country in 1899.

II Bloomfield Ranch

DRIVE on down through the sage for a couple of miles. Just before you reach the grade along the creek, far to the right against the hill, is what remains of the Jim Powers homestead. This is now the east portion of the Bloomfield ranch. The few old, gnarled pear trees were part of the original Powers ranch.

Jim Powers, the son of a '49er, first came to the Valley in 1879. After working for W. W. Landers almost a year, as a cowboy, he went to work for Thomas H. Smith. On July 4, 1880, Jim married Smith's daughter, Henrietta, and they were soon settled on this old ranch in the upper end of the Valley. Henrietta had been afflicted with infantile paralysis since birth and even though crippled, bore Jim fourteen children in eighteen years—all single births.

6   James Henry Powers, 1880.

When Mrs. Powers died in 1898, some say she died in self-defense. Two of the oldest girls, who were fifteen and eighteen, helped raise the family until death took them in their early twenties. Diseases, such as diphtheria, made serious inroads in large families, and only five boys and three girls of the Powers family lived to maturity. Charley, the oldest boy, took the ranch over in the early 1900's and raised a family of three boys and three girls. When they became high school age the family moved to Bakersfield where Charley took a job for the city. The boys were Stanley, Wesley, and Wayne; the girls Evelyn, Elenore, and Virginia.

Preston did a little mining and ranching, but worked most of his life for the U.S. Forest Service. One of his first jobs for this agency was to help Walt Cline and Frank Apalatea build a cabin for the Forest Service at Cannell Meadows in the high country. He and his wife, Betty, raised a boy and two girls.

Jack Powers ranched all his life, and at seventy-nine years of age he had completed his fifty-fifth year of running cattle in the South Fork Valley and on the Mojave Desert. His addition to the Powers family was a boy and a girl, Donald and Mildred.

Marvin, Jim's fourth son, lived his entire life on the South Fork, where he raised cattle. He was also State Cattle Inspector for fifteen years. Marvin will be covered more completely in a later chapter.

The youngest son, Kinnie, ranched for many years before he went to work for the State Highway Department. He and his wife, Daisy, had one boy who died in his teens, and another who died as an infant. The oldest girl, Clara, married Willy Nicolls, and this family will be covered later. Jessie married Earl Phillips, and there were a boy and a girl, Chuck and Bernice, born to this union. The youngest of the family was

Ettie and, as her mother died giving birth to her, she was raised by her grandmother. When she grew up, she married Elsworth Johnson and they had one son, Lloyd, spending most of their married lives in the Bakersfield area.

In 1900, the Sierra Forest Reserve, whose head office was in Visalia, California, employed Jim Powers as a forest ranger for the southwest division of that forest. Jim had lost a large part of his cattle herd in 1898 from a severe drought and was trying to build back the herd. The older boys were able to handle the cattle, and the pay of sixty dollars a month that he received from the Department of the Interior was about twice what he could receive working for most ranches.

Although the exact boundaries of his division are not known, the area he patroled extended from Little Lake on the Mojave Desert, to Dove Springs Pass. He patroled the area west through Kelso and the Piute Mountains to Walkers Basin, where he also conducted Reserve business. He also worked in and around the towns of Havilah, Isabella, Keyesville and Kernville, as well as the whole South Fork Valley.

Jim furnished his own riding horse and pack horse, and each night would camp either in one of his many camps scattered over the country, or stay overnight with friends. He was home several times a week and usually on Sunday, which was his day off. Some nights he would spend at his old ranch, which he spoke of as the Upper South Kern. He received his instructions through the mail from Forest Supervisor Newhall, and mailed his reports in monthly.

Jim had a variety of jobs, but the one that seemed to take the most time was keeping track of the many bands of sheep that crossed the Reserve. The history of American sheep grazing is very old, and many natural landmarks were named after the sheepherders, such as Sirretta Peak, Bartolas Mountain and Manter Meadow. Around 1900 the Government decided that cattle were better suited to the Forest, and sheep were excluded except where they crossed through the Reserve.

As these bands of sheep came down the Mojave Desert it seemed they were drawn by a magnet to wander off the prearranged driveway and feed further and further up the desert canyons until one of the rangers put them on the

Powers family—1894. *Left to right*, Druzilla, Mrs. Powers, Charlie. Mattie, and Sophia (*in front*).

Henrietta Powers, 1880.

7

Ranger Station at Indian Creek—1900.

right track. Citations were issued for trespass, but the best way seemed to be in escorting them through the Reserve lands. Many of the bands turned west over Walker Pass and traveled down through the Kern River country by way of the old sheep drive over Greenhorn Mountain. Some of the names of the owners of these early bands of woolies were John Ramond, Juan Ansolabehere, Joe Eyraud, and Pete Garard and his brothers.

Jim usually worked alone, although he occasionally mentions in his reports of meeting one of the rangers from an adjoining division, such as Burton, Hilton or Anderson.

A few of the entries from his daily diary are included to give the reader some idea of the broad scope that a ranger's work covered in 1900:

Nov. 22, 1900—Left Indian Wells at 7 A.M., traveled on road to Coyote Holes. Found that two bands of sheep had gone south towards Mojave. Overtook the owner, instructed him about traveling through the Reserve, then came north through Walkers Pass. Found one band there, talked with him and came in to South Fork to get horse feed. Arrived 5:30 P.M. Miles traveled: 30. (At this time of year he had to carry barley on his pack horse to feed his stock as there was no other feed available. In the spring he could hobble his stock or stake them out on a long rope when he camped at night. Most spots he camped in had no corrals or fences.)

Dec. 9, 1900—Left Indian Wells at 6:30 A.M., went to Coyote Holes. Left my camp there, then traveled through the desert to Bird Springs. Put off the "Reserve" four bands belonging to Olcese and returned to Coyote Holes. Arrived 6 P.M. Miles traveled: 40.

Feb. 22, 1901 — Left Upper South Kern at 8:00 A.M. Traveled on trail to Lamont Meadows Tsp 36, Range 25, Sec. 25. Examined trail to see what work was needed and returned the same way. (This trail is parallel to the Chimney Peak Recreation now.) Miles traveled: 35.

May 17, 1901 — Left Landers Ranch (in Kelso Valley) in company with John Weldon. Traveled east on south line of Reserve to near Gold Hill, found 3 bands of sheep inside the Reserve, put them out and returned. Arrived 5 P.M. Miles traveled: 24.

May 18, 1901—Left Landers Ranch at 7 A.M. Traveled east on south line of Reserve to Dove Springs, looking for sheep, and returned by way of Saint John Mine to Kelsey Valley. (Now called Kelso Valley.) Arrived at 6 P.M. Miles traveled: 25.

May 28, 1901—Left Isabella at 7:30 A.M. Traveled up the Kern River 8 miles and marked some mining timbers for Alison and Gibson and returned to Kernville. Arrived 6 P.M. Miles traveled: 25.

May 30, 1901—Left Stavert's Ranch (just below what is now Wofford Heights) at 7 A.M. via Isabella. Traveled up Bodfish Canyon to Glenolive and Polkadot mines. Interviewed some men and returned to Smith Ranch. Miles traveled: 40.

June 13, 1901—Left Smith's at 7 A.M. via Onyx and Weldon. Interviewed some cattlemen who were moving cattle through the Reserve to Monache Meadows, then took the trail to camp in Piute Mountains. (This trail goes

Sheep on the Mojave Desert.

Jack Powers, pioneer cattleman, taken in 1915.

south into the hills from where the Kernville cut-off road hits Highway 178.) Arrived 7 P.M. Miles traveled: 35.

JUNE 21, 1901—Left camp at 8 A.M. Traveled on road W. Rankin's place (this was in Walker's Basin) to inquire about cattle coming from Caliente and returned to camp. Arrived at 4 P.M. Miles traveled: 10.

JUNE 22, 1901 — Left camp at 8 A.M. Rode to Lightners by N. J. Williams. Filled out permit. Returned to camp at 5:30. Miles traveled: 12.

JULY 1, 1901—Left Dove Springs at 7 A.M. Traveled on road to Desert Springs to see if Briggs cattle were there. Met John McCray and went to Kelsey Valley. Arrived 10 P.M. Miles traveled: 35.

JULY 6, 1901—Left Smith's at 4 A.M. via Onyx and Sageland to camp on Piute Mountains. Arrived at 5 P.M. Miles traveled: 35.

JULY 15, 1901—Left camp at 7:30. Traveled north through T. 28 and T. 27 via Wilkstaff Meadow (now known as Woolstaff Meadows) to Rocky Point to see what work was necessary on the old trail leading through there and returned. Arrived at 6 P.M. Miles traveled: 30.

JULY 16, 1901—Left camp at 8 A.M. Traveled on south line 6 miles then north 3 miles to Sage-

land to interview some miners and returned by the Burning Moscow mines. Arrived 5 P.M. Miles traveled: 20.

JULY 25, 1901—Left camp at 7:30 and traveled on the road to Bright Star Mine. Settled some business with J. B. Ferris about cutting some timber on the Reserve and returned to camp. Arrived 4:30. Miles traveled: 12.

AUGUST 8, 1901—Left Smith's at 7 A.M. Traveled south over Scodie Mountain. Came down to Butterbredt's ranch. Remained overnight. Arrived 6 P.M. Miles traveled: 20.

AUGUST 26, 1901—Left Smith's at 7:30 A.M. Traveled on road to J. V. Robert's place to locate land. Returned to Onyx. Saw fire on Greenhorn Mountain, rode over there and helped put out fire. Arrived 10 P.M. Miles traveled: 35.

AUGUST 31, 1901 — Left French Meadow at 7:30. Down Kelsey Creek by way of Burning Moscow and Sageland to my home near the Smith Ranch. Arrived at 5 P.M. Miles traveled: 30.

DECEMBER 12, 1901—Left Smith's at 7 A.M. in the company with U.S. Deputy Marshall to locate Juan Etchevverry. Found him at John Nicoll's Ranch and returned to Upper South Kern. Arrived 3 P.M. Miles traveled: 16.

JANUARY 8, 1902—Left Cross's place at 8 A.M. Traveled west on north side of river to Patterson's Lane, crossed bridge on south side of river via Weldon and Onyx to Smith's Ranch. Arrived 5 P.M. Miles traveled: 18.

JANUARY 15, 1902—Left Chimney Meadows at 8 A.M. Rode west to summit of range. Looked over to South Fork of Kern River, saw smoke (this was in Rockhouse Basin), rode to where it was and found a pine log burning. Fixed it so it couldn't spread and camped. Arrived 5:30 P.M. Miles traveled: 16.

JANUARY 16, 1902—Left camp at 8 A.M. Rode up South Kern by way of Canada Meadows (now called Kennedy Meadows) and returned by trail to Chimney Meadows. Arrived 6 P.M. Miles traveled: 25.

FEBRUARY 7, 1902 — Left Isabella at 7 A.M. Traveled on road to Kernville, interviewed H. L. Cook about his permit for cutting fence posts, then traveled up river 4 miles to see Jim Stavert about cutting Cook's posts. Arrived 3 P.M. Remained overnight. Miles traveled: 15.

The Rankin home on the Bloomfield Ranch, in the early 1900's. *Right foreground*, barns and corrals.

FEBRUARY 8, 1902—Left Mill Town at 7 A.M. via Kernville, up South Kern to Smith's Ranch. Arrived 5 P.M. Miles traveled: 15. (Mill Town was located just below where the Kern Valley Golf Course is now.)

FEBRUARY 19, 1902—Left Upper South Kern at 8 A.M. Rode to Onyx and returned to Smith's to sharpen tools. Was quarantined there by Health Officer of Kern County for smallpox.

MARCH 17, 1902—Left home at 7 A.M. Traveled on road via Onyx and Weldon to Isabella to meet Supt. Newhall. Then to Kernville and returned as far as O'Brien's place. Arrived 6:30 P.M. Miles traveled: 34.

MARCH 19, 1902—Left home at 7 A.M. Rode up Kelsey Canyon to Pinyon Mountain and Gold Hill to look about some Mexican miners who are working there. Talked with them and returned to Butterbredt's Ranch. Arrived 6 P.M. Miles traveled: 36.

MARCH 21, 1902—Left Smith's at 8 A.M. Traveled on road via Onyx to John McCray's to see him on cattle business, then to John Nicoll's and to W. W. Landers and returned to Smith's Arrived 4 P.M. Miles traveled: 24.

The preceding is an example of the type of work Jim Powers did as he made his rounds. A small amount of time was spent at his home base — just enough time to shoe his horses, sharpen his tools and make out monthly reports. He put a lot of miles on his horses, but he fed them and took care of them in the best possible manner. Jim had raised most of his horses from colts, as he had several brood mares and a thoroughbred stud named Woodberry. The fine blood lines from this horse continued for many years in the South Fork.

Jim's herd of cattle were building back, so he quit the Forest Reserve to give his attention to his cattle. It seems his work was appreciated, as in September 1902, just four months after he had resigned, the Forest Service supervisor offered him a similar job with a raise of $30 per month. This would have been a very good salary, but he chose to stick to his cattle. A 1904 permit shows that he took four hundred head of cattle into the Forest, branded with the Circle Dot, which was the family brand.

A line of cottonwoods and greenery that grew against the rocky hillside was irrigated by water leaking from the old wooden flume, built for Powers by Jeff Gilliam in 1890. The series of ditches and cedar troughs were far from watertight. In fact, two-thirds of the water leaked out before it reached the spot where it was most needed. The dripping water encouraged the growth of underbrush along the route of the flume, creating terrain of brush and rocks ideally suited to rattlesnakes. This constituted a real hazard for ranch hands who hacked their way through the dense growth to repair and clean the troughs and ditches.

Sixty years or so of digging out accumulated silt, and throwing the debris along the sides of the irrigation system, resulted in banks seven or eight feet high in places.

In 1915 Jim wanted room to expand his operation and take his boys into the cattle business with him and so sold out, moving to Old Mexico. His plans were never realized as he died and was buried there.

The Bloomfield Ranch is second on the right to the river water, preceded only by the Smith ditch, and is thus assured of abundant irrigation for its many acres of excellent soil. James Pruitt first filed on this ranch in 1872, and the family names that come to mind in connection with ownership of this ranch include Rankin, Hutchison, Thomas and Gardner, in that order.

III Coogan's Cabin

NORTH of the Bloomfield Ranch lies one of the roughest sections of country in the West. Part of this is the Dome Land Wilderness, an area of the Sequoia National Forest set aside by the President to assure its remaining wild forever. Noted for the spectacular rock dome formation, it defies all but the most hardy.

That section of the South Fork of the Kern River that winds from Rockhouse Basin to Highway 178 is by far the greatest challenge left today for sportsmen in the southern end of the Sierras.

For generations before the coming of the white man, the local Indian tribes frequented these banks during their annual migration to the high country. Evidence of their sojourn there can still be found in many locations. In the late 1800's and early 1900's prospectors, in their quest for gold, pushed back into this extremely rough country. One of these venturesome individuals was Preston Powers who, as early as 1910, set up a camp where Manter Creek empties into the river. This wide place in the canyon gorge for some unknown reason was dubbed Tea Flat.

Preston had found a rich placer deposit in the gravels of the Kern and, although troubled by the blue clay that defied separation from the gold, he worked his claim quite profitably for some time. Preston was occasionally visited by several members of his family. One of these was his younger brother, Marvin, who was so impressed by the beauty and good fishing in that spot that even after fifty some odd years of running cattle in the high country he still talked about his stay there. The lure of this primitive section was passed on to Marvin's children. In 1969 Marvin's grandson, Kenneth Powers, also thrilled to pulling fighting rainbow trout from the waters of the South Fork at that exact location.

Following the miners into this area were cowboys such as Jack Powers and John Nicoll. They worked this drainage once or twice each year to take out cattle that had drifted in. They did not encourage their stock to use this country as it was quite easy for the cattle to become wild if they remained there too long. This happened in many cases. There are still stories being told today of the wild rides and chases when a cow on the prod would become the aggressor, creating some hazardous situations. In a few cases, getting them back to the ranch so they could be used for meat could only be accomplished by shooting them and packing them out on mules.

Until 1921 only the locals enjoyed this spot. In that year Kenneth and Chester Wortley started a pack station on the edge of the Mojave Desert at Sand Canyon and began packing parties into the South Fork gorge. They soon built a reputation for top flight stock and guide service. Among their patrons that first year was Cecil B. DeMille. The year 1922 brought a cloudburst and flood that completely wiped out their Sand Canyon headquarters. They moved to Nine Mile Canyon. As the road ended where the Los Angeles Aqueduct crosses the canyon, they built three miles of road beyond this point to their new base. From here they packed such notables as Walt Disney, then a young man of twenty-one years of age, and Jessie L. Laskey, into the back country. In 1923 Jackie Coogan and his parents also took these trips. Jackie was at this time a child star nine years old, and this proved to be just the spot the Coogans were looking for to get their son away from the pressures of filmland. Jackie had just completed "The Kid" with Charlie Chaplin. At the time he received a check for $500,000 as a bonus. The area so impressed the Coogans that they contacted the Wortleys that winter to build them a cabin at Tea Flat.

Coogan's Cabin, taken in 1925 when the first group of boys arrived in camp.

The trip into what was thereafter called Coogan's Cabin entailed two hard days' ride, with the first night being spent in camp at Lamont Meadows. Before the cabin and furnishings were completed, over eight hundred mule loads traveled this tortuous trail. The cabin was built of native logs, and water was piped in from nearby Manter Creek. The huge rock fireplace, a garden, and milk cows made this spot as luxurious as any outpost of that day.

In 1925, wanting to make a one-day trip possible into Coogan's Cabin, the Wortleys moved to the Bloomfield Ranch, and proceeded to tackle the almost impossible job of building a trail up the west side of the river. As Ken Wortley described the trail, it seemed more for goats than horses and mules. Part of their new development was a summer camp for boys. Again, not to do anything halfway, they arrived with a group of boys, most of whom were enrolled in the F. Curtis School, and whose names were connected with many of the most prominent people of the '20s and '30s. Here, in part, is a list of those remembered:

John and Richard DeMille—sons of Cecil B. DeMille.
Andrew Mellon—grandson of Andrew Mellon, Secretary of Treasury.
Jimmie Rogers—son of Will Rogers.
Bill and Jess Laskey — sons of Jessie L. Laskey.
Loren Grey—son of Zane Grey.
Noah Beery, Jr.—nephew of Wallace Beery.

Allen and Jerry Phipps — sons of Senator Phipps of Colorado.
Adolph Coors—heir of the Coors estate.
Andrew McLaghlen — son of Victor McLaghlen, actor.
Tim Holt—son of Jack Holt, actor.
Henry Mudd—son of Harvey Mudd, mining.
Lawrence and Larry Barker—sons of Barker Brothers.
Jack Sinclair—grandson of Texas oil tycoon.
Carlos, Walter, and Gus Robinson — of the J. B. Robinson Company.
Don Levey—son of Donald L. Levey, Insurance Company.
Bill and Ed Janss—sons of founder of Janss Investment Company.

and, of course, Jackie Coogan.

The crew was outfitted at the Bloomfield Ranch and off into the wilds they went. Over one hundred head of horses and mules were required. Various locals, such as Cecil Pascoe of Kernville, furnished stock for this impressive string. As noted previously, the trail could definitely not meet today's standards and was anything but safe. No word of any casualty, though, has come down through the years.

Ken and Chester had a full crew on the payroll, and one of those who cooked was Bill Beaty. Once at the camp, eating, fishing and

Paul Rhoads packing out of Fairview—1928.

swimming seemed to be the favorite pastimes, along with the normal amount of horseplay. One of the tricks pulled on the boys that will long be remembered was that of a "buried treasure." We all know what any boy would give to find a buried treasure. Some adults contrived the following. A treasure map was drawn up, using old scars on trees, and other natural landmarks. It was made to look authentic, even to the most skeptical. The map was stuffed in an old bottle and, when the boys were in the middle of their afternoon swim, down the rapids and into the swimming hole it floated.

Noah Beery was the first to grab the bottle and claim exclusive rights to the find. He was soon off in mad haste with the rest hot on his heels. Any one of them would have given anything to have possession of that map. A little bigger than the rest, Noah managed to stay ahead. But when he got to where the treasure was supposedly buried, they closed in like a pack of hungry wolves. Not one to be intimidated, he pushed and shoved until they gave him the room he needed to realize his find. The men had taken an old metal box and buried it a short way underground and, as Beery's frantically digging hands uncovered it, a gasp went up from the group. Pulling it from the hole, he forced it open. Inside was a piece of cardboard with one penciled word, "stung." It was kind of hard on the boy for a while but, as always, they seem to live through such disasters.

Among other things enjoyed by the boys at Coogan's Cabin was the study of Indian lore.

Zane Grey in 1924.

This had been a favorite camping spot for Indians. Numerous arrowheads were found, and the boys helped Ken rebuild an old Indian trail which worked its way up on Black Mountain to the west. All in all, it made for memories that will never be forgotten by those who participated.

The Wortley brothers continued to build their reputation as packers and, for a while, packed parties up the North Fork of the Kern from Fairview. In the fall of 1928 they packed out 345 legal bucks. The bag was then two bucks per hunter, and many of the pack trains came in with ten to twelve big bucks. Many of these deer came from around Paloma Meadows and the Trout Creek areas.

From Fairview they packed in some of the early Sierra Club groups. Several of these groups

Sierra Club Party—Picture, taken in 1928, while on a trip from Fairview to Mount Whitney and return. *In the front row* are some of the packers. *From left to right,* Loren Mack, Gerald Mack, Ken Wortley, Tom Allred, John the cook, Paul Rhoads, Pete Labachotte and, *far right,* Joe Loveall.

Ken Wortley enjoys his retirement at his home in Black Gulch.

totaled over eighty people, using up to 150 head of stock. The Wortleys employed sixteen veteran packers. Joe Loveall and Paul Rhoads were among these. Again the Hollywood notables continued to pick Wortley's outfit to pack them into the high country. Such names as Robert Stack, Anna Q. Nilsson, Hal Roach, George Holmes and Frank Garbutt went up the trails with Ken and Chester.

For sixteen years the Wortleys spent their winters with Zane Grey and Jessie L. Laskey, visiting spots from Alaska to the South Seas and Panama. From 1924 to 1930 they went down the Colorado River in canoes and down the Balsis River in Mexico. They were the first known white men to travel the Balsis waters.

Zane Grey, who had western novels and short stories on the best seller list from 1917 to 1925, made total sales of nineteen million dollars. He was most famous for his *Riders of the Purple Sage*. In one of his books he used Ken and Chester as the main characters. Zane sums up their qualifications in a recommendation given them in 1928, which follows:

"I can heartily recommend Chester and Kenneth Wortley in any capacity whatever, pertaining to camp life, woodcraft, pack trains, saddle horses, etc. They have been on expeditions with me to Arizona, to the Mexican coast and Galapagos Islands. They are also gentlemen, well-educated, and splendidly equipped to take care of people in the mountains."

The Wortley combination was broken up in the late 1930's by the untimely passing of Chester. While Ken still packed until 1965, he did not have the same interest in it. He noted that "the type of people we packed into the mountains in the '20s and '30s have all searched out new frontiers, such as Alaska and Africa, where they can fly in." Ken returned to public life for a while when, beginning in 1954 he published the monthly *Sierra Rainbow* magazine. Ken interviewed many of the true oldtimers who have since gone across the Great Divide. And, many of the stories were based on personal experiences in the back country that Ken loved so well.

The Coogan's Cabin area of the South Fork was, some fifty years later, just as wild and unspoiled as when Jackie Coogan pulled his first fish from the pot holes along the river. The cabin, just a heap of rubble with only the corner standing, is now used only for a wandering bruin to sharpen his claws. I suppose this wild, picturesque canyon remains for someone to come along as talented and resourceful as the Wortley brothers to open up another pack train into this spot.

IV The Land and the Water

WATER from the South Fork of the Kern River is the lifeblood of the land through which it flows. In 1970, as with their predecessors one hundred years ago, ranchers such as the Smiths at Onyx have no wells. They rely entirely on the river as their source of water. Each pioneer rancher went far enough up the river to make the water run in contour ditches to the portions of land he wished to irrigate. A crude dam would be formed at this point. In some cases, a cottonwood felled across the stream in the right place would back water up enough to force it down the ditch in the spring of the year. Later, as the river went down, other measures were employed to obtain additional water.

One method of constructing a dam was to cut green poles eight feet or so long and drive them into the sand of the river bed behind the logs or trees. Poles were then lashed lengthwise across the previous foundation, after which a layer of small limbs, gourd vines, and old hay would be applied. The last part of the operation involved taking a two-horse Fresno scraper into the river and cutting out a channel. Each load of sand was dumped against the dam. As the water continued to rise, the team was often required to swim for a short distance with the driver being dragged along by the lines. In some years, because of the lack of snow in the high country, many streams ceased to flow. Such was the case in 1885 when the South Fork of the Kern River decreased to a mere trickle. The case looked hopeless until someone remembered that fifty air miles to the north, high in the mountains of the Sierras, two creeks ran parallel. One of these, Golden Trout Creek, formed a portion of the headwaters of the main Kern and bordered against the headwaters of the South Fork. At one point these two streams are three hundred and fifty feet apart, separated only by a small ridge. Plans were laid to build a tunnel, thereby borrowing a little water from Golden Trout Creek and subsequently, the main Kern. Once this action was decided on, all haste was made by the ranchers to complete the project. Fifty air miles turned into seventy-five miles by trail as there were no roads in that part of the country. Loading powder, caps, and all the necessary tools and food supplies on mules, they started out. The trip was made in four days. The ranchers camped at Chimney Meadows, at the head of Nine Mile Canyon, Kennedy Meadows on the South Fork, Smith Meadow on Fish Creek, and finally arrived at what is now known as Tunnel Meadow. In those days one tried hard to remember all that was needed, as stores were not immediately at hand.

Although it was no small chore, the ranchers soon had driven a six foot by six foot tunnel through the three-hundred-fifty feet separating the two streams. But the ground was too sandy, and before water could be taken through, most of the tunnel caved in. Not to be stopped this easily, they gave a Valley resident, Jeff Gilliam, known for his ditch building ability, a contract to make an open cut of the tunnel. This he did, by means of teams and Fresno scrapers. The ditch was finished, but was never brought down to grade, so a dam had to be thrown across Golden Trout Creek to force water through the cut. For a time this upset Mother Nature's plan as to the headwater division of these two streams.

In 1895 Miller and Lux, the Kern County Land Company, and affiliated companies filed a suit asking for a court order to prevent the South Fork ranchers from using this water, but it was never pressed to trial. In 1901 and 1908 similar suits were filed but they were never completely decided on by the courts. In later years the ditch between the two streams was

15

Lottie and Ed Pettypool—1896.

abandoned because of maintenance costs. Remains of the ditch can still be found and, as long as its trace remains, it will stand as mute evidence of the resourcefulness of the pioneer ranchers.

The section of the ranch located west of the road—on the straight stretch approached by Bloomfield Grade—was originally settled in 1859 by J. V. Roberts, the first Caucasian to live in the Valley. Roberts came here from Walker's Basin, married one of the local Indian women, and settled down to family life. Many of the early Valley settlers took Indian wives and established families that were and still are a credit to the community.

A few head of rangy, wild cattle that Roberts brought to the Valley formed the basis of the beef business of which William Weldon became a partner. Roberts and Weldon butchered several times a week and loaded the meat on pack horses for delivery to the mining camps. As Roberts prospered, he started to loan money with interest. There were no banks in the Valley. When someone was short of ready cash, Roberts was the man to see. After necessary arrangements were completed, Roberts dug up the cash box he kept buried in the back yard. That yard has been the site of a prodigious amount of energetic digging in the years since Roberts died. Many have cherished the hope that he may have forgotten something. So far, the indications are that he took it with him.

In 1907, when John Cuddeback and John Cross bought the Powers cattle, they went to Roberts for the money. Clifford Cross, as a boy, went along with them to the Roberts place and

16

remembered waiting in the house while Roberts disappeared outside for a time and returned with the cash to buy five hundred head of cattle.

Roberts was also the first on the South Fork to take water from the river to irrigate. This was in 1860. The next was William Scodie in 1861. At this time the river ran in a narrow, shallow channel. During the 1861-62 winter one of the worst floods in history swept through the South Fork, creating a much wider and deeper channel and making it much harder to withdraw water for crops. In 1863 John Nicoll and Thomas H. Smith developed their ditches. In 1970 their heirs are still using these water rights on the original claims. In 1866 Jesus Miranda built a ditch and used this water on land that lies just below where the Kernville short-cut road crosses the South Fork. After another major flood in 1867-68, the following ranchers filed for their water rights: William and John Carden developed what was called the McCray ditch. James Prewitt took water out on what is now the Bloomfield, and the Mack, O'Brien and Miller ditches were also established. In 1870 W. W. Landers purchased the claims of Morgan and Scott, thus gaining title to water later known as Lander's ditch.

In 1871 James Grant took out water rights on what was known as the Grant ditch. In the same year, the Andress, Petersen, and Swan

Left to right, Nellie and Gertrude Pettypool with Jumbo, in the early 1900's.

ditches were started. The year 1873 marked the first use of the river water by Arthur Cannell. In 1874 Charles S. Collins settled on the land owned by Glen Alexander in 1970 and took out rights for his ditch. The same year the Mill or Hillside ditch was built. The Wirth, Cottonwood and Murphy ditches received water rights in 1877 and in 1885 the Robinson Brothers and Fugitt ditches were taken out. As it was in the past and is today, water from the South Fork is literally the life blood of ranches scattered throughout this Valley.

Immediately to the south of the Roberts place—now part of the Bloomfield Ranch—is land homesteaded by Bill Chico, an Indian. Chico's descendants still own the land.

A gentle rise in the highway brings you out onto another flat which spreads out from both sides of the road. This is Cap Canyon, named for Captain Edwin Andress, who homesteaded a ranch east along the river in 1878.

Ed Pettypool married Captain Andress' daughter, Lottie, in 1896. The couple lived in the house built by the Captain. In 1970 Mrs. Pettypool was ninety years old and still living in the Valley. She told of the rebuilding and repairing that Ed did around the old house. She was especially proud of the two-foot by three-foot by six-inch granite slab that Ed cut for a hearthstone. On it he carved a ten-inch star and the date "1896" to commemorate the date of their marriage.

V Smith Ranch

THE old Andress place is now part of the Smith Ranch. As you pass Tex Oliver's Ranch House Estates, the Smith place spreads out for more than a mile behind you and ahead for three miles between the road and the river.

Fields were all named by the pioneers, and the last one along the road as you go down has been called, since 1882, the School House Field. The Scodie School was established in this year at its western edge. The only evidence that remains is a setback in the fence, and some of the old cottonwood trees that still shade the ground. Some of the teachers who will be long remembered for having taught there are Emma Johnson, 1882; Ella "Miriam" Smith, 1886-91; and Mrs. Mabel Lowell, in 1903. Those who attended this school had many happy memories, such as holding one's hand across the spout of the pump at the school yard well while a friend pumped you a drink, or boys running out and stopping the old peddler's Model T Ford by pulling on the back bumper until the engine died. The children came from as far away as the Powers Ranch on the upper end of the Bloomfield Ranch, which was five miles. Walk-

ing, riding horses or in their buggies or buckboards, they filed in to learn the three R's. Many of the Indian children and some of the whites also, preferred to go barefoot the year around, and developed callouses a quarter of an inch thick. A few stories tell of the Indian boys skating on small ice ponds barefoot.

This stretch of road, so close to the hill, does not receive much sun during the winter period so, a fire was built early each school day and was maintained throughout the day. One of the favorite pastimes at recess was climbing the rocky mountain to the south. Most of the children seemed as agile as mountain goats.

When Thomas Hooper Smith founded the ranch in 1861, he set aside a portion of the land for use as a family cemetery. This is the quaint old burial ground nestled in a curve of the hill and was named Cottage Grove Cemetery after the Smith Home. A walk through the tree-shaded serenity of the cemetery may give a lesson in local history to those who take time to read the weathered inscriptions on the gravestones. In front of the cemetery is an old tree stump encased in rock and glass. The tree, planted by Smith in 1862, succumbed to the

Ella "Meriam" Smith taken at the Scodie School in 1890. *Left to right, back row,* Ida Thomas, Janie Roberts, Martha Roberts, Sarah Thomas, Pearl Johnson, Elsie Stahlacker, Lizzie Thatcher, Ollie Thatcher. *Front row,* Daisy Batz, Druzie Powers, Charlie Powers, Druzie Thomas, Ella Smith, Pete Chico, Fred Thatcher.

Cottage Grove Cemetery on Highway No. 178.

Old cottonwood tree planted by Thomas H. Smith in 1862.

18

Scodie School, 1919. *Left to right, on first horse in back,* Chuck Phillips; *front,* Clayton Ripley; *second horse,* Lloyd Tungate, *back;* Billie Rankin, *front; third horse back,* Evelyn Powers, Tungate girl, Eleanor Powers, Gladys Jenkins. *Standing in back,* Chico boy, Virginia Powers; *front, left to right,* Margaret McDonald, Margaret Anderson, Ruth Anderson, Stanley McDonald, Sterling Tungate, unidentified, Miss Campbell (teacher), Leroy Rankin; *and on last horse,* Allen Doyle.

Scodie School, taken in 1902. *Back row, left to right,* Clara Powers, Helen Skinner, Johnnie Powers; *second row, left to right,* Hattie Smith, Jessie Powers, Neva Chrysler, Preston Powers, Victor Powers, Antonio Chico; *front row, left to right,* Marvin Powers, Sr., and Stanley Smith.

Sophia Maria Smith, the first white woman to live on the South Fork. Taken around 1860.

ravages of time after providing a century of shade for Valley mourners. The present monument was built by one of Smith's great-grand-sons as a tribute to the memory of his pioneer forebears.

One-fourth mile below the cemetery, as the highway curves sharply, you will see the Cottage Grove Home, as the Smith house was called in the early days. When Thomas H. Smith brought his wife, Sophia Maria, and their three small children to the Valley, she was the first white woman to live on the South Fork. Indian women would come for miles to see the White Squaw.

Mrs. Smith started a tradition of family hospitality that has prevailed down through the years, as she served tea to these early visitors.

There were no doctors in the country for many years, and Sophia served as midwife and physician for many years. With her supply of patent medicines she was always available when needed. No exact records were kept of the number of babies she helped bring into the world but they were many, including three for her oldest daugnter, Sophia; three for her daughter-in-law, Ella; and fourteen for her youngest daughter, Henrietta.

In the 1800's Sophia's husband, Thomas, was badly crippled. He had been out during a snow storm, cutting down cottonwood trees so the cattle could eat the leaves, when a tree fell on him. This accident made it necessary for Sophia to take over much of the running of the ranch. In the early days she drove a horse and buggy to the mining town of Havilah where she sold eggs and fresh garden produce raised on the ranch. The Smith home became the center of community life in the Valley. It was the scene of weddings, births and solemn occasions of death. The first ice cream socials to be held on the South Fork were also held here. Its doors were never closed to friend or stranger, and many a traveler camped overnight in the yard and was sped on his way with gifts from the Smith's ever-full larder.

19

It was this type of hospitality that averted disaster one day in 1875. A rough bunch of Mexicans rode into the Smith's yard. As was his custom, Mr. Smith greeted them and asked them to share a meal with the family. Mr. Smith was able to converse with them in Spanish as he had spent several years in South America. They declined the offer, and he overheard one of them who seemed to be the leader say in Spanish, "We have met a gentleman; we will not rob this place." It was later discovered that the one who had made this statement was none other than Cleovaro Chavez, who had been the lieutenant of the infamous Tiburcio Vasquez. After Vasquez had been hanged, Chavez had taken over the leadership of his gang and this group of bandits, having robbed William Scodie just half an hour previously, also intended to rob the Smiths.

Down the way a few hundred yards from the Smith place is the home built by John Butler Batz in the 1880's. J. B., as all the natives called him, came to California in 1874, and first worked for William Landers for almost three years. Next he clerked for J. J. Murphy in Kernville for fifteen months, then worked three years as a clerk for I. Michel's Big Blue Mine Store. During this time he married Sophia Smith, daughter of Thomas H. Smith at Onyx. J. B. built a home for his bride in Kernville and, as he had left home and learned the carpentry trade at age fifteen, he was able to do all the work himself, making the doors, sash, etc. by hand.

Thomas H. and Sophia Smith—1910.

He went into business for himself, and located on a 240-acre ranch, which later became the property of William Kissack, Sr. After the ranch became successful he sold it to Patrick O'Brien and moved his family back to Onyx, where he took up 160 acres west of the Smith Ranch. Besides doing a small amount of ranching, he also clerked for William Scodie until 1888, when he was appointed Undersheriff of Kern County under Sheriff W. J. Graham for two years, 1889-1890.

J. B. then returned to Bakersfield to take over the post of County Treasurer. He held this post until 1903. At this time he helped form the Bakersfield Abstract Company, and became its first president. The whole family became involved in this venture. J. H. Jordan, who had married his daughter Daisy, became the first vice-president and his son, Vernon, was also employed by this company.

Living room of the Cottage Grove Home, where all the weddings and funerals were held. Wall rack holds cylinder records for the old Victrola, and Mrs. Smith's picture hangs over the piano.

The Jim Powers family moved into the Batz home in 1898, when Mrs. Powers died, and it was later known as the Powers Place. It was here, in 1916, that the first South Fork Women's Club meeting was held. The old home was still being used for a dwelling some ninety years after it was built, which attests to the carpentry skill of J. B. Batz.

The second Mrs. Smith to live in the Cottage Grove home was Ella, wife of Tommy Smith, and she also was a very unusual person. Best known in later years as Grandmother Smith, she was deeply loved by all who came into contact with her. In the 1890's, when her three children, Hattie, Stanley and Helen were small, she wrote the following list of "Things To Do and Remember," and it gives the reader a small glimpse into her true character:

THINGS TO DO OR REMEMBER

1. Have S. S. (Sunday School).
2. Prayer meeting at Mr. Smith's
3. King's Sons & Daughter's Circle.
4. Parties for the children.
5. Reading room and do away with drink on Sunday.
6. Say grace before meals and read the Bible in the evening if the rest do not object.
7. Syringe childrens' ears with a little alum in water.

Mr. and Mrs. J. B. Batz and daughter, Daisy, taken in 1888.

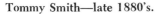

Tommy Smith—late 1880's.

8. Read the Bible by topics and study books of the Bible from a general standpoint.
9. Flour and molasses poultice for boils.
10. Put vinegar in dried applesauce and pies.
12. Have Sunday pastimes for children at home like building Noah's ark, etc.
13. To oil a floor take linseed oil and turpentine and apply three times with a rag.
14. One good Sunday pastime is making maps out of damp sand or clay or modeling Bible characters and objects in clay.
15. King's Daughters Circle have fairs, do mending and sewing, have social times, help build church.
16. Keep Sunday reading on hand.
17. Chemistry and science for a farm. Books on subject. Interest for children.

21

Children of Tommy and Ella Smith. *Top to bottom,* **Hattie, Stanley, and Helen.**

18. Give high thoughts at the breakfast table; a noble story, a noble thought. Lead children and others' thoughts away from *self* and *gossip* to talk and think of things.

19. Say "come" to our children and not "go." Lead them, not push them.

20. Things to make meetings interesting — Spelling matches, history games, geography games, evenings with authors, biographies and readings, anecdotes about them, divide history into epochs, take one at a time and great characters of the times, etc. Women authors.

21. Miss Clark's "Ever Faithfuls." Go to a house of a member or otherwise and sew all afternoon for $ .10 a piece. The fund to go toward church improvements, etc. Gentlemen could belong but have no say. Pay dues and fine of $ .10 when coming to a meeting. Ladies fine $ .10 when staying away.

22. Sewing and quilting bees, apple-paring bees, etc. Gardening bees at the schoolhouse.

23. King's Daughters pay fines for slang, etc.

24. Borax for bed-bugs, cockroaches, etc.

25. Give children in a home Bible answers to questions that will be asked him in his life and rules to go by and comforting passages for times of discouragement. Have them learn verses, learn pieces of poetry, hymns, etc. on Sunday. Ask and answer questions at family worship.

26. Sing the old grand hymns — "How Firm a Foundation," etc.

27. Have verses on a special topic.

28. Try not to get behind the times for my children's sakes.

29. Teach girls *caution* and both boys and girls to remember.

30. Do not crush the manhood and womanhood out of boys and girls. Trust them in all you can.

31. Burn camphor for mosquitoes.

32. A child's soul is of more importance than his clothes. If I have not time to pay enough attention to both I will neglect housework or clothes rather than the child's intellectual or moral well-being.

33. Grab-bags with presents for children. Grab-bags with words or questions in teaching.

34. Advice to a mother while carrying child:
    1. Practice self-control and shake off morbid feelings.
    2. Diet on ripe fruits, milk, lamb, veal, fowl.
    3. Exercise by taking walk in fresh air in mornings. Not stand on feet too much.
    4. Sleep much.
    5. For morning sickness take warm drink before getting up in morning and take magnesia in water.

35. Sunday scrap books for children. Take any pictures and put Bible verses underneath to correspond to pictures.

36. Two teaspoonsful of powdered tannin to one teaspoonful of glycerine for babys eyes.

37. For diarrhoea in infants, 1 cupful oatmeal to 2½ quarts of water and salt. Boil 5 hours, then sweeten.

38. Feed babies regularly. Two hour intervals, increase to four hours.

39. Double piece of cotton flannel 2½ yards for a bath-blanket.

40. Topic Party is a good pastime for some evening. Have subjects on programme and choose partners for subjects.

41. A good idea is the saving of scraps of all our dresses and making an album of them.

42. Keep a diary of wild-flowers where and when found year after year.

43. Grace for a baby's lips:

"For these and all Thy gifts of love
We give Thee thanks and praise.
Look down, oh Father, from above,
And bless us all our days."

44. Make picture puzzles by pasting pictures on cardboard and then cutting up in pieces.

45. Work as one Christian Endeavor Society in country did:

Started S. S. schools in districts around, held song-service in schoolhouses Sunday evening. This opened the way for special services by pastor. Song service meant plenty of good singing, Scripture reading, prayer, sermon read by a good reader, also a poem on the subject read. More singing.

46. Best & Co., Liliputian Bazaar, 60-62 West 23rd St., New York. Juvenile Novelties.

47. Be interested in everything my children bring to me that they may not drift away from me, and may always confide in me.

48. Teach them to give to God and the poor by requiring it of them in their childhood.

49. Some ways of amusing a company of people.

1. Chopped proverbs. Sentences from some book of proverbs written on a slip of paper and then cut in two and the pieces pinned around the room and each one looks for one he thinks he can match. The one who gets the most books (four pieces make a book) gets the prize and least a booby prize.

2. Tea Test. Questions, the answer to which must be a word ending in the sound "t".

3. Questions for conversation on queer shaped cards and then the card cut in two and one piece given to a lady and another to a gentleman. They hunt for the one who has the complement to their question and then converse for ten minutes on the question.

50. Comfort bags to make at meeting out of strong gingham or cretonne for men in lumber or mining camps, containing thread, needles, etc.

Tommy and Ella raised their children on this old ranch, where the girls as well as Stanley worked in the hay fields and went to the mountains with the cattle. Stanley and Hattie both married and raised their families on the South

Weaver Hand repairing a horse-drawn mower—1916.

Fork, only Helen moved away, marrying Bill Brown, a banker from San Francisco. She and Bill raised a daughter Barbara, and a son Rodger, in that city.

This Smith home gained a reputation for culinary excellence almost as soon as it was established. Ella carried it on, and Mrs. Stanley Smith was still carrying it on in 1970.

When the Smiths first came to the South Fork they raised only garden produce; they later started raising hay to feed their stock in the winter. Prior to 1870 grain hay was the primary crop. In that year alfalfa was introduced by Jack Waterworth on the Landers ranch and quickly became the leading source of stock feed.

In the early days, haying was primarily a hand operation. A scythe with a three-foot curved blade was used to cut the grain, after which men with pitchforks formed it into shocks. After three or four days in the shock it was loaded by hand onto a flat bed wagon, on which it was hauled away to be stacked. Stacking was also done with pitchforks, with the height of the stacks determined by the distance upward a man could pitch. A little later a gin pole with a swinging arm was used to lift the hay off the wagon in a net, and raise it up on the stack.

Compare these crude methods, requiring many men, teams and man hours, to those used on some of the ranches on the South Fork in 1970.

One man goes into a field with a machine called a swather, which cuts and rakes the hay in one operation. After four or five days the

Tony Chico on Jackson rake—1915.

same man returns and bales the hay with an automatic baler. Then a loader, operated by the same lone man, picks the bales off the ground and stacks them on a flat bed trailer. The bales are hauled to the stacking site, where the entire trailer bed tilts vertically, neatly releasing the bales, which have never been touched by hand.

In this way one man can put up more hay in twenty days than could fifty men using the old methods. These methods described below, used by the early settlers to put up their hay, including the care and feeding of ranch hands, was typical of most of the ranches of the area. Ranchers there many times pooled their manpower at haying time. Crews, composed of men from the various ranches, moved from place to place until the hay was put up.

Haying hands at the Smith Ranch slept at first in a dormitory type room that was the top story of the house. After 1928 the old Scodie School was moved down to the ranch and used for a bunkhouse. It was built in 1882 and was originally located about one-half mile up the road from the Smith place.

Daybreak on the Smith Ranch was announced by the vigorous application of an iron bar to a great iron triangle that hung outside the kitchen door. The men washed up for breakfast at a wash-bench on the back porch. A couple of washbasins and a bar of home made soap comprised the facilities. Water was provided by a handy pitcher pump, which also was the supply for the house. A piece of broken mirror fastened to the wall above the bench added to the general tone of the setting. Why it was always a broken mirror is anybody's guess, but it always was. An entire, uncracked, unblem-

ished one never got as far as the bunkhouse wash bench. An endless roller towel was still on the porch in 1970. A cow's tail hung nearby to serve as a comb cleaner, alongside a comb suspended on a string for those who may have misplaced their own.

The second ringing of the triangle was the signal to head for the kitchen. As in all the old ranch homes, the kitchen was the most used room in the house. The saying was that "the front door hasn't been used in so long, folks coming to visit wouldn't recognize it if they saw it." The kitchen door became the main entrance, as the widening of the highway eliminated the front gate.

In the old days the main feature of the 12-feet by 20-feet kitchen was a huge wood-burning stove. This has since been replaced by a 1936 electric range. However, the 3-feet by 12-feet table remains in almost the exact center of the room.

Haying hands were not much for small talk. Once seated at the table, eating proceeded in dead earnest, perhaps interrupted by someone poking fun at one of the younger men who, the night before, had made a ten-mile round trip on horseback to see his girl.

The quality of the food served was excellent and the quantity was prodigious. Cooked mush was included on the menu always, though it was usually passed up for more succulent edibles such as huge platters of ham, bacon or sausage from the ranch smokehouse; eggs, boiled, fried or scrambled; pots of pink beans which were served at every meal; hot cakes or biscuits; milk gravy; butter; jam and jelly.

Chili peppers, tabasco sauce and chile tepinos, those little peppers that look like Spanish peanuts and can taste like molten lava if used too unsparingly, were provided especially for the Indian hands.

The meal was washed down and topped off with huge cups of steaming, black, strong, boiled coffee—unpercolated, undripolated and unSilexed. Wonderful!

As the sun started over the rocky hills to the east, the men headed for the barn to catch and harness the teams. Mules were preferred to horses because they could be used to pack supplies into the mountains between hay cuttings. As many as seven teams were employed in the first part of the haying operation; four for the mowers and three for the Jackson rakes.

The mowing machine had a five-foot cutter bar. The blade or sickle slid back and forth inside these guards, something like hedge clippers. Power was supplied by a gearbox run off the wheels of the mower. One of the older men was usually kept busy sharpening these sickle bars on a grinding wheel. The wheel was provided with a seat and powered by a man's foot on the pedals. Water in a can suspended above the wheel was adjusted to drip on the grindstone and keep it cool.

A field is cut from the outside in, as you would peel an apple. When the mower operator approached the center of the spiral he would climb down and try to flush out anything that may have run before the blade and was hidden in the tall hay. This maneuver was performed in a gingerly fashion. Skunks and snakes are not fit company for a busy man.

Anything in the path of the mower was destined to be chopped up, of course. Small animals, birds, rattlesnakes—all were victims, so to speak. Once in a while a skunk got in the way of the cutter, thus posing the question of who was being victimized by whom. The mower operator was rendered unfit for social purposes, subject to an immediate change of clothes and the next meal or so eaten outside. The mower itself remained aromatic for several days.

After the hay was cut and left to wilt for a day, men with Jackson or sulky rakes would pull the hay into windrows, then go down the windrows and rake it into shocks six feet across and three feet high.

Many colorful anecdotes are told of the Jackson rake teams. The rake was very lightweight. Sometimes the driver would get down for a drink of water and off would run the mules, creating havoc among the newly raked windrows. This is why many of the hands kept a gallon water jug wrapped in a gunny sack on the piece of equipment. If the outside were kept damp, the water stayed cool even on the warmest days.

Sometimes, owing to social activities the previous night, a rake operator might be less alert than usual. Tony Pablo had his team run away with him one time. When the going got rough,

The stately cottonwood trees that are so much a part of the South Fork Valley provide the shade for the noon meal brought out in a horse drawn buggy. This group of old timers snapped in 1915 are, *left to right*, Weaver Hand, Marvin Powers Sr., Ray Cross, Burro Smith, Earl Phillips, Marvin Cross, and Tony Chico.

Tony either jumped or was thrown off; he doesn't remember which. Anyway, the rake missed him completely, but the wheel cut off one of his ears.

The noon meal, or dinner, was every bit as epic as breakfast. The steadfast rule "good food and plenty of it" prevailed. Food was brought in a horse-drawn buggy to the fields by the women and was eaten in the shade of the cottonwoods along the ditch banks.

Cold chicken was always featured, along with sandwiches of ham, egg, roast beef or pork on home-baked bread. Dessert was pie, cake, cookies or home-grown fresh fruit, including watermelon.

Accompanied by gallons of water with lime juice (bottles now collectors' items) such a meal was guaranteed to fill any chinks or hollows acquired since morning. After about 1920, milk was added to the noon meal. A little digestive time was spent in relaxed conversation under the trees or simply watching clouds of blackbirds swooping through the sunny fields—these are memories still cherished by those who recall the good old days.

Most ranchers of the Old School say that stacked hay beats baled hay a hundred ways from Sunday, when it is to be used right on the ranch and not shipped out or moved around. Stacking time gave the experts a chance to show their stuff; some of the oldtimers had been stacking hay for fifty or sixty years.

Haying crew on Smith Ranch, stacking loose hay.

The stacks were built about twenty feet square and thirty feet high. As ragged and uncoordinated as loose hay is, a stack put up by three or four men who knew their business was a sight to behold. Each man worked on his own corner. The finished project would be as square as a box, with sides perfectly straight up to where the top started to form a rounded top.

One of the many good stackers on the South Fork was an Indian by the name of Mike Phillips, known to most as Canebrake Mike. In 1945 he was approximately ninety years old and still stacking hay. Mike weighed only one hundred pounds or so, but he could handle tons of hay in a day, rolling and pushing it into place with a pitchfork. If you asked Mike how long he had lived in the Valley he would answer, "come a long time ago—no mountains then."

Mike lived in a little shack on the southeast side of Canebrake Flat. He cut oak wood with an axe and gathered piñon nuts, selling the wood and nuts to local residents to supplement the money earned at haying time. Regardless of the season, when Mike needed meat he would take his rifle south into the Scodie Mountains, returning two or three hours later with the meat from the deer he had shot all boned out and tied up in the skin slung across his shoulders. What he couldn't use fresh, he would use for venison jerky.

At the time of his death, Canebrake Mike was close to 115 years old.

Many Indians worked in the hay fields. They were expert stackers and teamsters and were unsurpassed in what they called "Indian irri-

gating." The land was so irregular and undulating that the irrigator had to know exactly where and how long to turn the water on from each place on the ditch. The Indians had irrigated the same fields for so many years that they knew each high spot and swale as well as they knew anything in life.

These same gents were usually peerless horsemen, working cattle on the open range when not otherwise occupied on the ranch. Family names of Indian ranch hands on the South Fork recur on payroll records through the years. They include Andreas, Bencoma, Chico, Mace, Pablo, Miranda and Cisternas. Tony Pablo is an old time hand who still rode and worked cattle on the South Fork in 1970.

One oldtimer who was a good stacker was Burro Smith, who became known as "the human mole." For the final fifty years of his life, Smith spent every winter tunneling through a mountain on the Mojave. He worked the hay fields each summer to get his grubstake to enable him to dig a little further. Smith's tunnel did not lead anywhere in particular. He just had a notion that he wanted to dig through a mountain and he did, all the way through. Quite a feat for one man. Who is to question another man's goal in life?

Jim Kerruish was another stacker of note. Jim, a bachelor, came here from the Isle of Man and bought the True place below Onyx. He ran his own ranch, but was always willing to help his neighbors. Two other oldtimers who were excellent teamsters and stackers were Paul Rhoads and Earl Phillips.

The present Stanley Smith was one of the best, and this is borne out in the following account. Once in the 1920's the three men on the stack weren't quite able to keep up with three buckrakes, or at least someone complained about being rushed and suggested they might use a fourth man. Stanley said "why, I could handle that job by myself." The men promptly climbed down, and Stanley took over. They tried their best to cover him up or make him holler quits. The three buckrake teams were in a lather when they finally conceded that he could do it by himself. Here again it was a matter of experience, and many times just as a load was to hit the stack, he would stick his fork into it and push and rake the whole mass to the exact spot he wanted it, instead of moving it in ten or fifteen forkfulls, the way others might.

Sand burrs took a lot of the fun out of stacking. A stackerload of hay full of these little jewels would sometimes fall on the back of one of the stackers. Nothing to do but call time out and holler for somebody to come help pick stickers.

Every so often a live rattlesnake was picked up with the hay by the buckrake and carried to the stack. The distinctive noise made by the rattle would occasion some high and fancy stepping on the part of the men on the stack. Men have been known to become airborne from the top of the stack in their eagerness to leave the area to Mr. Snake for as long as he wanted it.

Two or three buckrakes were used to bring the hay to the stack. The eight foot long wooden teeth of the rake, ten teeth per rake, spaced about a foot apart, skimmed along the ground picking up the loose shocks of hay. When a load was achieved, the driver pulled back a wooden lever, which raised the rake about eight inches off the ground. The load then rode to the stack on the three small iron wheels, one mounted under the driver's seat and one on either side, behind and beneath the teeth. The center wheel pivoted, to allow for backing and turning.

A skittish team has accounted for many a wild ride on this unusual conveyance. The only recourse for a driver in such a predicament was to continue picking up hay until the load was so heavy that the team was unable to run with it.

For many years the Jackson stacker was the favorite of South Fork ranchers, though later

Earl Phillips on buckrake.

Canebrake Mike, Tubatulabul Indian, was still stacking hay at 90 years of age.

superseded by the overshot. In the early 1900's, Earl Phillips introduced a system using a pole and net to convey the hay to the top of the stack. This was tried for a while on the Smith Ranch, but was abandoned in favor of the overshot.

The overshot stacker had a set of teeth which corresponded with those on the buckrake. The team pushed their load of hay onto the teeth of the stacker, and the load was lowered. The stacker driver drove a long pole into the ground

27

Marvin Powers Sr. operates horse drawn buckrake. Pole and net were used to lift loose hay up on stack.

behind the hay to keep it on the stacker, and the buckrake was backed off. The stacker team, hitched to a fifty-foot cable, was driven out, and the load was raised on forty-foot arms up and over, to be dumped on the stack. A load was stacked every ten minutes or so. With three good men, usually two in front and one in back stacking, everything went smoothly. As the hay stack reached the required height, the men would gradually form it into a peak or rounded top. When properly done, this peaked formation would shed rain water like a thatched roof.

One of the many incidents remembered by the haying crews on the Smith Place began when one of the Powers boys, who was stacking, asked Kenneth Rhoads, the stacker driver, to toss up a canteen of water. Rhoads' toss came up short of the necessary twenty feet, and the canteen fell back, hitting the rump of one of the stacker team horses. Although usually a gentle team, this so startled the horses that they took off down the path before Rhoads could grab the lines. The front of the buckrake, that had just begun unloading onto the stacker, rose four feet off the ground and crashed back to earth. This, in turn, caused the team on the buckrake to panic, tangle up in its harness, and fairly tear the buckrake to pieces. The sudden pull on the cable by the stacker propelled the load to the top of the stack with the speed of a rocket, where it hit the stops with a crash, showering hay all over the men.

In a frantic effort to get away, the stacker horses would lunge forward, hit the end of the cable with such force that they were jerked violently backward six or eight feet, then plunge ahead again. Their intent was to escape the whip-cracking, cursing and yelling going on behind them. Each time the team would lunge, the stacker mechanism would hit the stops with a bang, causing the men at the top of the stack to fear that the entire stacker was about to topple over on them. In time, the horses were subdued, and things slowly assumed some semblance of order. Powers, who had called for the canteen, surveyed the now peaceful scene for a quiet moment, then remarked, "All I wanted was a drink of water."

As may be seen by the previous descriptions of haying time meals, food in vast quantities loomed large in the minds of all concerned. The work of harvest was extremely strenuous; men laboring a long day in the fields required a great deal of fuel in the form of substantial, rib-sticking food to keep them going. To the women of the South Fork ranches, it was a point of pride to create good-tasting, nourishing meals for many hands. Most of the food was home-produced except for flour, salt, green coffee, tea leaves, and sugar. A ranch with a reputation for generous amounts of delicious edibles never lacked for willing workers.

All meat served at the Smith Ranch was raised and processed on the premises. A typical supper for hay hands included beef steak or beef roast, ham, roast pork or pork chops, or

Overshot stacker is moved from one stacking location to the next. Cables are clamped when stacker teeth are off the ground. Two small wheels on one end and timbers shaped like sled runners on the other, enable the stacker to be dragged by a team.

perhaps a beef stew. Potatoes, boiled in their jackets or fried, and the ever-present pink beans that held down the more delicate garden fresh or home-canned vegetables, at least two kinds, that always graced the table. Mounds of fresh butter, also home-made, were slathered on thick slices of home-baked bread. A fellow who had already had seconds and was, perhaps, self-conscious about reaching for thirds, might fill in the crannies with bread and rich, thick gravy before helping himself to dessert of pie or cake. Few hands were noted for their timidity at the table. Home-grown and canned fruit was on the table at every meal, as were gallons of cold milk and hot coffee. Haying hands were not royalty, but they ate at least as well as the average king.

Hay is still being raised on the Smith Ranch, and the same good meals are still the order of the day. But with fewer and fewer men experienced with horses, mules and pitchforks, haying has become mechanized, and automatic balers have replaced the cable-operated stackers.

Some of the old hands attempted the transition from mule to machine. Most of them found that a hay hook felt strange in their hands after so many years wielding a pitchfork. They would sit in the shade of the cottonwood trees that dot the South Fork, and a stray breeze might bring them the odor of fresh mowed hay which still has the same sweet perfume it did in the 1800's, and they would reminisce on how it was to go out to the field behind a team, a good breakfast under their belt, and work with the jingle of harness chains and the clatter of mowing machines in their ears.

The advent of modern haying methods not only meant that fewer men were required to do the job, it also meant that a great deal of the charm and romance went out of one of the areas of ranch life of those families who still put up hay on the South Fork of the Kern River.

VI Johnny Powers

ALTHOUGH there was generally a good working relationship between ranch owners and their hired hands on the South Fork, an incident occurred in the summer of 1891 that showed problems did arise.

The trouble started this way. An Indian by the name of Wampei Jiggens, while working on the Smith Ranch, had broken a pitchfork handle. Young Tommy Smith, feeling that he had broken it on purpose, informed Jiggens that the price of the handle would be taken out of his wages. Wampei, who camped in Sage Canyon, was a member of a tribe of Shoshone led by a chief named Kiowa. Wampei was well-known for his surly disposition, and his own mother once admitted that he had killed his two half-brothers. This tribe of Indians, which had moved in from the Panamint Mountains, weren't too popular on the South Fork. Although a few of them did occasionally work for the ranchers of the Valley, they were generally avoided even by the local Indians. They seemed content to scratch out a living from a rich vein of gold-bearing quartz—rich enough that even in the 1970's descendants of early Valley residents search for it. Jiggens, after a few harsh words with Smith, drew his pay and paid a visit to Scodie's store before starting back to his tribal rancheria.

It was this trip to the store that probably greatly influenced Jiggens' behavior for the next few days, for, while there he got hold of a quantity of the hard stuff. Whiskey in those days was not supposed to be sold to Indians, but somehow it often managed to reach the hands of those who wanted it. One rumored source of supply was a small trap door built in the wall behind Scodie's Store counter. Local pioneers tell of seeing the following happen. A dusky hand would reach in with a silver dollar and

Constable Johnny Powers—1890.

Scodie, or one of his clerks, such as Louie Bowers, would push a bottle of bootleg whiskey over to where the grasping fingers could safely pull it outside to waiting lips. Maybe this opening only served to let Scodie's cats in and out of the store. But, for sure, Jiggens did get a large amount of whiskey that day, which prompted the following actions.

As he trudged up the road past the Smith Ranch on his way back to the tribe, he had to go right by numerous hay stacks that loomed high in the moonlight. As the whiskey had further increased his dislike for anything that looked like hay, and for the Smiths in general, it wasn't long before three stacks were glowing torches lighting up the whole mountainside. As the stacks were about a half mile from the

ranch house, all three were completely consumed before anything could be done. Jiggens had quietly slipped away in the dark.

The constable at Onyx at this time was Johnny Powers. Johnny, who had come to South Fork as a cowhand to work for Bill Landers, had been appointed to the constable office. All the Powers boys were accomplished horsemen, which was not surprising considering that their father, John Washington Powers, was a stockman and the young men had been riding since childhood. But for Johnny being a working cowhand was no small feat, as he had lost his left leg in a shotgun accident as a small boy. This meant that he had to mount from the right side of a horse and those he rode were not the gentle kind you would find around a livery stable nowadays. Once aboard, he rode the roughest parts of the country after cattle as wild as deer, with his peg leg stuck jauntily through the stirrup leathers. His dark hair, good looks, and pleasing personality made him a popular favorite among men and women alike.

Thursday, July 2, 1891, Powers left Onyx with a warrant for Wampei Jiggens. Sam Gann, constable from Kernville, accompanied him.

They stopped for the night at Raymond's Station, then called Coyote Holes, which was owned and operated by Freeman S. Raymond. Employed at Raymond's Way Station at this time was the Widow Andress from the South Fork, and her four children: Jessie, 13—Lottie, 11—Ernie, 9—and Charlie, 7. Lottie Andress Pettypool, still living some 79 years after the incident, recounted the following.

Her mother tried to persuade Powers to wait until he had more help. She feared two men were not enough to apprehend Jiggens in his own territory. Young, healthy and self-confident, Johnny laughed off her warnings. His attitude was casual and "all in a day's work." Lottie said he came in from washing up, and quipped to her mother, "Mrs. Andress, you said you wanted my picture; well you can have the one I left out back on the towel."

The two constables started out for the Indian camp early the next morning. On the way they came on the camp of some coyote trappers. One by the name of Oliver McCoy said if they could wait until he finished breakfast he would ride with them. Before leaving, Powers deputized him, and all three continued south.

At seven o'clock they rode into the rancheria. Powers and Gann tied their horses up a short distance from the buildings, and McCoy rode right up to where Chief Kiowa had walked out to meet them. After some discussion, Kiowa said he would get his horse and help them look for Jiggens. But as he stepped back across a small ditch, and as if by some prearranged signal, one of the chief's sons stepped to the door of a shack and commenced firing upon the officers with a rifle. At this time Kiowa pulled a pistol from his shirt, and fired on the constables, who were caught completely off-guard. Although the three officers accounted for the chief, and two of his sons being killed after a short hot battle, Powers lay dead, and McCoy critically wounded. Gann, running out of ammunition and seeing no hope but to run for his life, caught McCoy's horse close by. Laying on the horse's neck at dead run, he managed to escape. It was later told by Jiggens' mother, through an interpreter, that upon finding McCoy still living Wampei set out to finish him off. When she tried to intervene, he told her to leave or he would also kill her. It is said that he slashed Powers' throat after he was dead, and further mutilated his body.

Gann covered the ten or twelve miles back to the stage station in record time. Lottie Pettypool remembers seeing him come over the pass to the south on his hard ridden, heavily lath-

Mrs. Andress.

ered horse. Raymond had a wagon load of wood he had gathered earlier, so, hiding the horse in the barn, and Gann under a canvas that was over the load, he set out for the South Fork.

Gann and Raymond were well on their way by the time five mounted bucks appeared in the pass, and after watching the station for some time, they rode warily down to the dwellings.

Mrs. Andress, with courage typical of women of her day, came to the door and asked them to come in and have something to eat, as she normally did. It was felt that her quick thinking probably saved her life and the lives of her little family. If she had shown fright or panic, they might have continued on their grisly massacre.

Bill Chico, veteran Indian tracker.

Mr. and Mrs. Freeman S. Raymond at Coyote Holes in 1906.

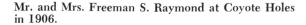

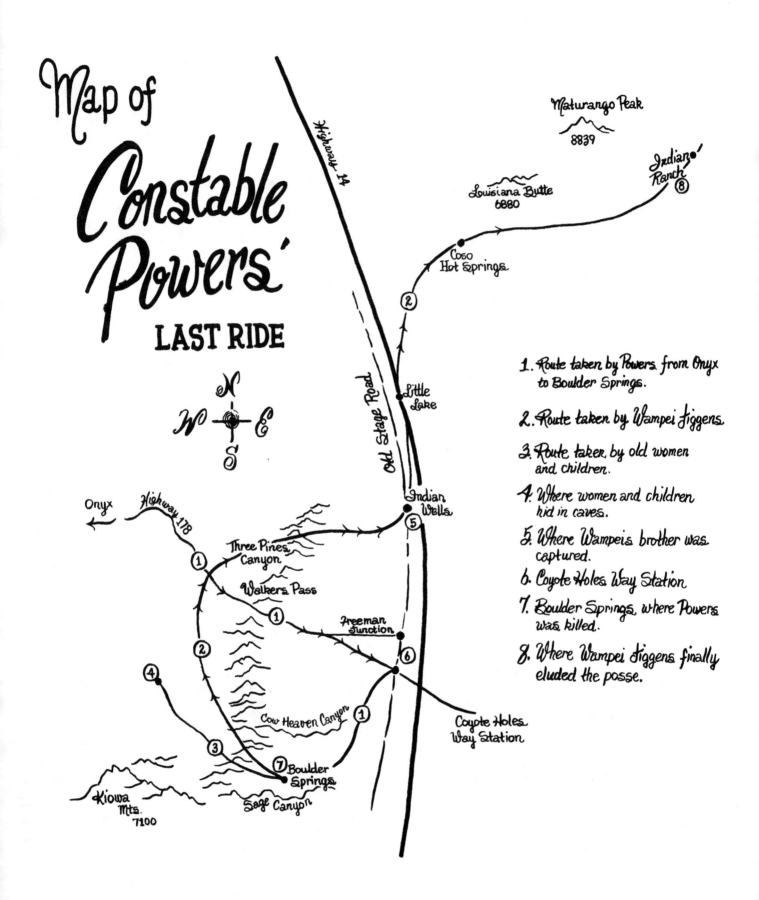

Map of Constable Powers' LAST RIDE

Maturango Peak
8839

Indian Ranch ⑧

Louisiana Butte
6880

Coso Hot Springs

Highway 14

②

Little Lake

Old Stage Road

Onyx

Highway 178

①

Three Pines Canyon

Walkers Pass

①

②

④

Freeman Junction

⑥

Cow Heaven Canyon

①

③

⑦ Boulder Springs

Sage Canyon

Kiowa Mts. 7100

Indian Wells

⑤

Coyote Holes Way Station

1. Route taken by Powers from Onyx to Boulder Springs.

2. Route taken by Wampei Jiggens.

3. Route taken by old women and children.

4. Where women and children hid in caves.

5. Where Wampei's brother was captured.

6. Coyote Holes Way Station

7. Boulder Springs, where Powers was killed.

8. Where Wampei Jiggens finally eluded the posse.

They replied that they wanted Raymond, and when she told them he had gone toward Walker's Pass to get wood, they rode off in that direction. Meeting the stationmaster on his return from delivering the survivor to the Valley, they gave him no trouble, since the load of wood seemed to back up his cook's story.

In the meantime, Gann's arrival at Onyx had the whole valley in an uproar. Though he didn't arrive until three in the afternoon, by four, eleven men were ready, and followed him back to the scene of the tragedy. At ten that night an additional twelve followed. In the posse were two local Indians who had relatives killed by Kiowa's band. One of these was Bill Chico. They took the lead, and meant business.

The posse reached Sage Canyon just after daybreak and immediately surrounded the rancheria. They were met by a most grisly scene. Lying in front of the house were the mutilated bodies of Powers and McCoy, which had been lying in the desert heat almost a full twenty-four hours. Powers' eyes had been punched out with his peg leg.

It soon became apparent that the Indians had moved out lock, stock and barrel. Just in case they later decided to come back, the posse made it as uninhabitable as possible — which included burning the buildings. As Gann was almost certain that Chief Kiowa, and at least one of his sons, were critically wounded when he took his hurried departure, they checked the area and, sure enough, found three graves. They proceeded to dig up the bodies and, although two wrongs never make a right, their remains were left exposed to the elements when the posse rode out on the trail of the Indian band.

These bones lay scattered among the sagebrush for many years. Some of the old time cowboys such as Willie Nicoll remembered seeing them through the years, until they finally disappeared.

The Indians, upon leaving their camp, had split in two parties. One group, mostly of squaws and children, after turning west up onto Scodie Mountain, hid in the rocks and eluded the posse.

The other half of the band turned north after taking to the mountains. A posse of twenty-three men, led by Deputy Sheriff Jim Powers, brother of the late Johnny Powers, were soon hot on their trail. Moving down on the west side of Walker's Pass, the Indians turned and went back out to the desert by way of the canyon back of James Station. Coming out in Indian Wells Canyon, they fled up the desert. By this time some of the posse had to return to their ranches. However, a full twenty men stayed with Powers two weeks as they played their deadly game of hide and seek in the desert country to the north. The terrain became increasingly more rugged each day, until Wampei and a few of the remaining men, shook the posse altogether.

The authorities around Lone Pine were also in on the hunt and, by keeping a sharp eye out for the offenders, were fast to arrest Jiggens when he showed up in town some three months later, wearing Johnny's constable badge pinned to his hat, and this was what led to his subsequent capture.

He was taken to Bakersfield, where he was tried in Superior Court, and on December 11, 1891, was sentenced to spend the rest of his natural life in the State Prison. Some of the South Fork residents were quite apprehensive of further outbreaks, but nothing more transpired.

One of the band, who at that time was a young boy, lived and worked on various South Fork ranches for many years. He had been crippled by a shot in the running battle.

Known only as Piñon John, he seemed destined to live his life out in peace, but one day in the 1940's he became involved in an argument with another Indian, and was clubbed to death with the butt of a pistol. An odd note is this. The other participant of this argument was Andy Chico, son of Bill Chico, the Indian who took a very active part in running down Kiowa's band.

VII Cattle King of the South Fork

A ROAD that turns right off the highway and crosses the South Fork of the Kern carries the sign of the Onyx Ranch headquarters. This ranch was established by three bachelors named Waterworth, Morgan and Scott. When Waterworth died, Morgan and Scott sold their claims to William Wallace Landers.

Very little has been written about Landers who, with the help of topnotch cowboys working for him, carved out a cattle empire during the early history of Kern County. This operation was exceeded in size only by cattle companies such as Miller and Lux and the Kern County Land Company. It was more typical of the earliest of the California cattle ranches than either of the former. As with most ranches of this period, Bill Landers depended completely on the range to sustain and fatten his herds, and raised only enough hay for the horses used in his cattle operation. Even the horses were fed hay only when they were on the home ranch.

William Wallace Landers was born in Texas in 1827. In 1850 he headed for California, driving a herd of longhorn cattle. It took him over a year to get to the Visalia area, where he ranged his herd until 1877. He then crossed over the Greenhorn Mountain and up the South Fork seeking feed for his expanding herd. There his headquarters were set up across the river from Scodie's Store at Onyx.

Landers first started ranging his cattle in Kelso Valley and on Scodie Mountain. Each year he expanded his operation to the south and east until by the 1890's his herds ranged south to Victorville, north to Little Lake and east to Death Valley.

Already established in the cattle business when Landers arrived was Thomas Hooper Smith, who ran his stock mainly to the north, in the Rockhouse Meadow and Kennedy Meadow area. Smith's cattle were, for the most part, descendants of the cattle from Spanish ranches to the south which had gone wild and had scattered into the hills.

Another of the earliest cattlemen was John McCray, who brought a herd of cattle across the plains in the 1850's. These were the first Durham cattle to come into California, and also the first blooded cattle to come into what is now Kern County. One of the earliest of the ranchers in this end of the San Joaquin Valley was Don David Alexander. Alexander had his headquarters at San Emidio about 1861. His 20,000 to 25,000 head of wild Spanish cattle ranged all over the San Emidio hills, around Kern and Buena Vista Lakes, and in the lower reaches of the Kern River. Alexander bought all of McCray's bull calves and gradually upgraded the quality of his herd. Walker Rankin, Sr., who settled in Walker's Basin in 1878 also used the McCray stock to improve his native Spanish cattle in Walker Basin.

In the early days it was the dream of most boys to ride for Bill Landers. Many of them were on their own, and were riding for this cattle king at what now seems to be a young age. One such lad was Add Cross who, in 1879, rode over Greenhorn from his Glennville home at the age of twelve to fill a man's job of working the open range. He stayed on to later become one of Landers' cow bosses. Add married Olla Beaty, a local girl, and raised six children. The three girls and three boys, in order of their ages, were Dell, Merle, twin boys Claude and Clifford, Nell and Jim. Clifford Cross, one of his offspring who lived in the Valley, will always be remembered as a cowboy of the old school— Clifford and his brother Claude also rode for

Ad Cross, old time cattleman, started riding for Landers at twelve years of age.

Willie Nicoll—expert with a rawhide reata—as he appeared when he rode for W. W. Landers.

Left to right, Claude and Clifford Cross, followed in their father's footsteps. They are pictured when they also rode for Landers in 1916.

Landers in 1917. Another youngster was Willie Nicoll who, at age fourteen, also left the home fires and became a full-fledged cowboy. Frank Apalatea not only was working for Landers by the time he was fifteen, but was later one of Landers' cow bosses.

Among those who held the coveted position of cow boss was John McCray, Jr., son of the man who brought the first blooded cattle to this area. Young John McCray came from Porterville in 1870 with Landers as a young man of seventeen. While cattle boss in the 1890's, his son Clint started with him on the roundups. It was during these grueling days on the desert range that Clint started accumulating the cow savvy which later prompted the Kern County Land Company to choose him as cattle superintendent — a position he held for thirty-five years. Other range bosses were Gene Rand, August Glade, Benny Roberts and Clayton Ripley, Landers' last cattle boss.

A person might slip by as a foreman on some jobs even if he was not an expert in his field, but not so with a cattle operation in those days. Men like McCray not only knew cattle and men, but had to be just a little tougher than any of their men. They were willing to ride the meanest horse in country almost too rough to walk through on foot, to bring out cattle as wild as deer. All the oldtimers who followed Landers' chuckwagon on these roundups cannot be entirely listed, but there were such names as

Three Landers cowboys stage a barroom fight for the benefit of the cameraman. Taken in 1910, they are, *left to right*, Charlie Powers, Bob Thomas, and Willie Nicoll.

Mark Lacy, August Glade, Pete and Frank Chico, Jake Pruitt, Johnny Johnson, Pete Labachotte, Clarence Cole, Red Vega, Earl McCay, and a number of Indians whose full names have been lost through time. One Indian was nicknamed "Red Eyed Pete," and another "Catfish Charley," so called because of his big mouth.

Oldtimers described the Landers' roundup as follows: The chuckwagon, pulled by four horses, would leave the ranch each spring and head down the desert on the way to the southern part of the range. The men would usually stop at Mojave on their way, and about twenty cowboys turned loose for a night in town usually livened things up considerably. More than once cowboys were not able to make it out of town on their own steam. The next morning they were loaded into the chuckwagon, where they rode until their heads went back into shape.

A herd of horses, or remuda as they were called, of seventy to eighty in number, was moved along with the wagon. More than one mountain lad got his start as a cowboy wrangling horses for Landers. As there were no fences, the horses had to be watched day and night. Although this job was nearly always delegated to a couple of youngsters, it created many problems that would even make a full fledged cowboy of today sit up and take notice. Some of the problems stemmed from the fact that most of these horses had been born and

raised with the wild bunch northeast of where Landers ran his cattle. Many of them retained a yearning throughout their life for that range, and would slip away if given half a chance. This range was called the Coso Mountains, and most of it is now within the Naval Ordnance Test Station at China Lake.

When the first white men came to Owens Valley there were herds of wild horses roaming the hills in the Coso Range. These mustangs dated back to the days when the Conquistadores brought horses with them to explore and tame the new world. It was the descendants of these horses that Landers used to build up his herd. Through the lack of care and inbreeding over the years these descendants had lost the quality of the original stock. But they retained a good share of the spirit and stamina. Their Coso Range took in a good part of the Malapi volcanic fields and, as a result, they were as sure-footed as goats and had excellent feet. Because of this, very few of them had to be shod.

Landers at one time in the late 1880's turned eighty registered Morgan mares out on this range and this, along with the shooting or castrating of the undesirable studs, caused a sharp upgrading in the quality of horseflesh that came out of the Cosos. Many bays resulted from this crossbreeding, and the average weight increased from 600 pounds to 1000 pounds, with a few reaching 1300 pounds.

Each year a crew would go to the Coso Range and round up the herds from several locations. In some cases they would turn gentle horses in with the wild ones. This made it easier to run the horses into traps or box canyons. They would then brand the year's crop of colts and alter the young stallions that they did not want to keep for breeding purposes. At this time they singled out horses to be broken. Generally they were allowed to run wild until they were four or five years old. Many times horses that eluded capture would be broken even after they had reached the age of ten. There are pros and cons about which age to start breaking a colt.

It seems there are many advantages to breaking older horses, especially with the mustang type or other cold-blooded horses. One thing for sure; when a horse reached four or five years of age and had not been touched by human hand except to be branded as a yearling, it took a pretty salty bronc-stomper to handle him. Stories still circulate of certain horses that dodged the horse runners year after year. One story was about a white stallion who had outfoxed cowboys for years. Finally Pete Labachotte, one of the old time mustangers, and a buddy managed by hook and crook to catch this wild one. Many times in the past this horse had jumped all fences put between him and the open range. This time though, he was corraled by a fence too high for even his flying hooves. Without a moment's hesitation, after realizing he had been trapped, he ran head-on into the stout log gate as if it was not there. In doing so, he broke his neck. It seemed as if he had decided to commit suicide rather than submit to capture and confinement.

Different methods of breaking horses were used, and I am not too sure whether they would work on today's hot-blooded breeds. At that time one of the accepted procedures was to rope a bronc by the front feet and throw him to the ground. He would be bridled and saddled, and when he got up he had a man on his back. If possible, the other cowboys would head the bronc toward a sandy creek bottom or plowed field, as this would work a lot of the hardest bucking out of him.

These horses had exceptional wind. The wild herds would lope for miles to and from water.

Pete Labachotte, one of the best of the old time mustangers. Taken in 1953 on his 70th birthday.

This stamina and sure-footedness put Landers' cowboys on good mounts when running wild cattle on the desert range.

Pete Labachotte was the leading character in a lot of the stories about wild horses of the Cosos. One story was that while after a wild horse, his own mount could not quite get him to within roping distance. He pulled up his horse, threw his saddle to the ground and proceeded again to give chase. Getting rid of the excess weight, plus the extra freedom of movement, gave his saddle horse enough speed. Then came the almost impossible feat of stopping eight hundred pounds of fury without a saddle. As Pete told it, it did not seem too hard. But the fact is that Pete was just one wild and woolly cowboy, and nothing was too hard when it came to stock. He had acquired the knack of flipping a half-hitch or noose up the rope to make a halter so the bronc would not be choked while he led him. This is a far cry from methods used today, where colts are halter broke and handled almost continually from birth until they are trained.

When the chuckwagon and all the cowboys reached the southern part of the range down around Victorville, the roundup started. The local cattlemen in the area would throw in with the Landers wagon, which furnished the grub for the whole outfit. Landers, in return, branded all the "big ears" or calves who had left their mothers, with his "L" brand. These were usually yearlings, but a number had escaped previous roundups and had gone unbranded for up to three years. By the time they reached this age they were as wild as March hares. There were some wild rides taken, and all caution was thrown to the wind to get them marked and branded.

The chuckwagon at dawn was alive with activity. The following is typical of this most colorful scene. The wrangler has just run the horses into a rope corral. This consists of only one rope being held waist high by the cowboys, as each man takes his turn entering and roping his horse for the day. They are led to an area close to the chuckwagon, where horses were unsaddled the day before. As each man saddles his horse, the picture livens up considerably. Things start happening. Out of twenty or more horses being ridden that day, there were always at least two or three that wanted nothing to do with the saddle. Even after being hobbled, they might tear up half an acre of ground before they are able to be saddled and made ready to go. As the men started to mount and get their broncs lined out for the day's work, what you were apt to see is mirrored in one of Charlie Russell's paintings, *Bronc at Breakfast Time*, where a cowboy is riding a bucking horse through camp, scattering things right and left. There is a lot of cursing and shouted threats from the cook, but he knows, as everyone else does, that there is no turning or directing a bucking horse. This is the high point of the day for many of the cowboys as they offer shouts of encouragement to the rider, and maybe a hat or two sails under the bronc to encourage him. If the undetermined course happened to take them through a bunch of yucca, they would get a big laugh from all hands, and several days of discomfort for the luckless rider as the punctures ran their course.

As the sun pops over the Superstition Mountains the cowboys head off in groups of five or six to where they split up to work the country scheduled for that day. Everyone knows what is expected, however, the cowboss issues a few brief instructions about who goes where.

As the day wears on, cattle start streaming into the pre-determined rodeo ground, and by late morning all the riders have been accounted for.

Many times the wrangler would bring the remuda out, and fresh horses would be caught for the rest of the work. A branding fire was built off to one side. Those calves belonging to the smaller cattlemen, such as the Cuddebacks, would be roped and branded first. When all these were accounted for, the rest—along with any "big ears"—would be branded for Landers. Branding was hot, dusty work; however, it was looked forward to as it gave the men a chance to show their skill with a reata.

When all the branded calves had trotted back to their mothers with smarting hides, cutting of the beef cattle began. Again, a lot of the men would rather cut cattle than eat. As with the branding, much of the success in putting on a good show and getting the job done quickly depended a great deal on the horse they were riding. These little mustangs took natur-

ally to cow work and a man had to have a deep seat in the saddle and many times grab the saddlehorn to stay with them as they dodged and turned to cut out the older steers. In many cases these steers had horn spreads of over five feet and weighed more than the horse. They had become rolling fat on the desert wild flowers and the sun glistening off their multicolored hides made these creatures a sight to behold.

With the branding and cutting of the beef finished, the main herd was turned loose to scatter onto the range. The "cut," or the beef cattle, were driven back to camp and included with those that had been cut during the previous days.

Each summer, as water became scarce and the desert feed dried up, these cattle were "stirred up and started towards the hills." These cows, having run on the same range for years, would travel from thirty to forty miles to the foothills or to their summer range. This included Kelso Valley, the Piutes, and Scodie Mountains. In November or December they would be pushed back out into the desert. This system did not always work. There are quite a few years recorded when because of lack of rain, there was hardly a blade of grass on either the mountain or desert range. In these years, such as 1898, great numbers of cattle died and you could ride for miles and never get the stench of rotting cattle out of your nostrils. Some ask why they did not drive them to feed, or ship feed their way. In those days a big steer would bring only seven or eight dollars. Even if you could find feed, the cost would be prohibitive.

The bad years hit large and small alike. Jim Powers lost 800 head on the desert in 1898. This comprised two thirds of his herd, but by 1910 he had built to his original number of 1200. So there is no way of telling how many head a cattleman such as Landers would lose in a year such as 1898. All they could do was borrow a little money, if they could, to buy beans and pay their riders for the following year. Tightening their belts a couple of notches and hoping the next few years would bring them out of debt occasionally worked.

The chuckwagon cook was a big part of the early cattle business, and his word was law in the vicinity of his cooking fire. Even the cowboss very seldom disputed his word, and the

Three South Fork fashion leaders in their Sunday best. *Left to right*, Bob Thomas riding Tule River, Charlie Powers on Stargo, and Willie Nicoll on Little Buck. Picture taken in 1910.

Frank Apalatea not only was a cattle boss for Landers but also rode for each succeeding owner through Rudnick and Alexander. Taken in the early 1900's.

cow hands—especially the younger members of the roundup—walked mighty light in the area of his domain.

Once in awhile someone might remark that the gravy was mighty salty, but would quickly add, "but that's just the way I like it." These cooks had a big job. Often they had a helper, but many times they would feed from fifteen to thirty men twice a day, in addition to moving the wagon every day or so and setting up camp again. Some of the cooks included Shorty Burnett, Phil Seybert, and Ed Gessell.

The meals eaten out of a tin pan while sitting on their bedroll by a sagebrush fire, made either favorable or unfavorable impressions on most of the old time cowboys. A cook that most remember was Louie Bowers, and here again different cowboys had different impressions of his culinary skills. Frank Apalatea said Louie was the "best cook I ever saw; always had hot grub whenever you came in, day or night." Pete Labachotte, on the other hand, was not so impressed with Louie, and noted that he was the "dirtiest cook I ever saw; spit right across the frying pan—didn't make it every time either. You know, one time I cut a stink bug right in two in the bread."

At best, the cooking conditions were anything but ideal. If the cook had a small table that hooked up to the tailgate of the wagon, he was lucky. Everything else had to be done on the ground. Different cooks might favor certain types of cooking, but most of them followed the same procedure in setting up their cooking

area. Generally, a six foot pit would be dug about a foot wide and eight inches deep. Greasewood was used mainly for fuel in the desert, and was hard to beat for cooking. When the fire had burned down to a three-inch bed of coals you had a good even heat that would last long enough to cook a meal. Some of the cooking was done on rods laid crossways over the fire pit, but most of it was done by sticking iron stakes in the ground vertically, on which another rod would be placed horizontally. From this the cooking vessels would hang with the aid of fire hooks, "short iron" rods crooked in the opposite direction at each end. The cooking equipment numbered four or five frying pans and as many Dutch ovens, a few kettles, and the ever present coffee pot. The Dutch oven (a large cast-iron pot with a rim on the lid to hold the coals) was the most used of any of the cooking paraphernalia.

Bread was baked for each meal and, to the cowboy, nothing would measure up to sourdough bread. The cook had his sourdough keg or crock, which he guarded with his life. This keg usually held about three gallons.

The sourdough batch was started by simply placing in the crock, flour, salt, and enough water to make a medium-thick batter. When this was well stirred, it was placed in a warm place for a couple of days to ferment. The good sourdough cooks said that you had to use sourdough at least twice a day to make it work the best. At each meal the cook would take out enough sourdough to make his bread, then add enough salt, flour, and water to always have plenty of working batter.

In making his bread he added to the sourdough batter more flour, a little soda, salt, and a generous amount of lard. After making sure that the soda and lard were thoroughly mixed in, he would pinch off pieces the size of an egg. These were then coated with hot grease and placed close to each other as possible in a pre-heated Dutch oven, as this made them lighter by rising more. The full oven was then placed beside the fire for about half an hour to rise. The cook put them on the coals at just the right time with a generous supply of coals on the lid so that this would finish cooking when the rest of the meal was done, as sourdough biscuits are best eaten hot.

Much of the mystery that surrounds a good sourdough cook comes from his knowledge of the right temperature to keep his working batter, and the fact that he used it at least twice a day. Most of the time the rest was just years of practice, and no recipe ever handed down seemed to get the results that those old boys achieved.

Even higher on the cowboy's list of necessities was his coffee, and the pot of about three-gallon size was always on the fire. The cowboy liked his coffee strong, and the usual recipe was a handful of coffee for each cup of water. The sight of the wide bottomed, smoke-blackened coffee pot on the coals, with the brown boiling

liquid overflowing down its sides, was a picture that would make the cowboy's mouth water. Although he drank huge quantities of this potent brew, it never seemed to keep him awake at night.

The first wagons that went out had on their bill of fare only meat, bread and coffee, then later beans were added, and the usual sight when the meal was being prepared was a black iron pot with cooking beans bubbling over the coals, which would whet the appetite of any man. In later years potatoes were used almost at every meal, and the wagon cook also started using canned goods. Canned tomatoes were the most popular, but some vegetables such as peas and corn were also used.

Plenty of good desert-raised beef was killed on the spot whenever the supply on hand ran out. They didn't age the beef, as they do now, but started eating it the day after it was killed. Much of the beef was fried, but stew got its share. Most often on the menu were plenty of boiled potatoes, although fried potatoes were common. The ever-present pink beans, and vegetables of peas or corn were included. Gravy that was made in the frying pan after the meat was cooked accompanied most meals. Sourdough bread, cooked in a Dutch oven, and coffee usually rounded out the meal unless some type of dried fruit was cooked up for dessert. These were the simplest of diets, but they seemed to stick to the ribs. It kept the cowboys going about their daily work, which was anything but light.

As an army marches on its mess kitchens, the cowboy works on his chuckwagon. Sometimes the cook would have a canvas fly hooked to the back of the wagon, but it usually wasn't enough to keep the blazing sun from baking his back and shoulders or the cold rain from soaking him. Regardless of all the drawbacks— wind that blew sand in the food, a shortage of wood, and a limited variety of foodstuffs on which to draw, these old boys still left reputations behind them that are hard to top. The type of riding done by these cowboys called for top physical condition, and those who did not have the needed vitality soon fell by the way.

Besides the two or three regular meals each day, the cook was expected to have something for the crew to eat when they went on duty for night herding. (The herding was mandatory since there were no fences.) The night was divided between two shifts, and all hands took their turn. When the men went on at midnight, a pot of beans or stew and plenty of coffee was kept warm by the fire so they could fill up before going out.

Cowboys of that era were a happy, carefree breed of men who worked and played hard. They had a lot of loyalty for the outfit for which they worked, and the men who rode with them. All the cow bosses previously mentioned seemed to get along well with their men, except for one by the name of Gene Rand. Rand tried to change a lot of things, especially methods of working the cattle. Both men and cows rebelled.

When he tried to change the locations where the cattle were to be gathered, the cattle continued to try to go to the old rodeo grounds, and this made for nothing but trouble. Some of the men tell about pranks being played on this boss, which are usually taboo around cattle people, such as spooking a thousand head of beef cattle and, in general, making life miserable for this boss. It was not long until he decided to move on, deciding that the South Fork of the Kern was not to his liking.

As the 19th Century drew to a close there were quite a few old pensioners around who had helped Landers build his cattle empire. Several of them usually could be found sitting either in the shade of the cottonwood trees by the blacksmith shop, in the bunkhouse, or on the porch of Scodie's store across the river. One of these included an old-timer by the name of Kent who, after Landers had pensioned him off, filled the job of postmaster at Onyx, and also had quite a bootleg operation going. Kent is rumored to be the one who originated the contraption known as the "cat hole" at the Onyx Store.

Another long-whiskered gent by the name of Gassy Taylor, so called for his story telling ability, also made the porch of the Onyx Store his daily headquarters. It seems he had saved a little nest egg working for Landers, in addition to making some shrewd investments. He kept a stake in the form of fifty dollar gold slugs, and would lend out money at fairly high interest. He did not believe in banks, so hid his money in a lard can. Once his hiding place was discovered. A hen ran cackling from under the bunkhouse, and one of the men started under in search of eggs for the Chinese cook. Gassy bustled up as he heard the commotion. He managed to deflect their efforts, and it was later learned that the hen had picked for her nesting spot the current location of Taylor's bank. Needless to say, Gassy moved his money to a safer place, this time burying it. There were still supposed to have been some of these gold slugs buried when he died, but repeated probing in the approximate area of the supposed hiding spot failed to turn up any.

An important part of the Landers holdings on the South Fork was the Mack Ranch, which Landers acquired from his friend, Henry L. Mack. The best part of the ranch was then, and still is in 1970, a large, natural meadow that stretches for a mile along the Kelso Valley Road. It was to this big meadow that the Landers cowboys would bring their beef each year, and buyers would come, usually from Bakersfield. They came by buggy, and would ride through the herds with Landers. After a lot of dickering they would agree on a price per head, such as $14.00 per head, or two cents per pound for a 700 pound steer. A price of $28,000 doesn't seem like much money for 2,000 fat steers, but operating expenses and taxes weren't so high in those years.

Most of the time cattle buyers would bring their own men in and drive the cattle straight from the ranch to the packing plants in Bakersfield. The sight of two thousand or more fat steers as they strung out for three or four miles is something that is still recalled by old-timers in the Valley. The cattle were driven down through the South Fork, up past Bodfish and Havilah, and finally came out into the San Joaquin Valley at what was then called Bena. They then crossed Bakersfield to the slaughter houses. Eight or ten good cowboys, well mounted, could handle a herd this size without too many problems.

On the edge of this same Mack Ranch Meadow, about half a mile from the Weldon cutoff and surrounded by large cottonwood trees, stood a line shack. Landers kept a man here during the summer months to keep an eye on the meadow and to pump water for the cattle when they were held over there. The power to bring the water to the tank was furnished by a blindfolded mule who went round and round at the end of a long pole called a sweep. John McCray told Jim Robinson about being at this shack for an all-night poker game in the 1800's. At daylight when the game broke up they had trouble pushing the door open. It had snowed more than two feet during the night.

When Landers passed away, his ranch was leased to Frank Boyce. After two years it was sold to Jack Doyle. Roland Hill also owned Landers' ranch for a time.

In 1932, Art Alexander, who had been the ranch foreman for the A. Brown Company for twenty-seven years, entered into a partnership with Oscar Rudnick to purchase the Landers ranch. They also bought from Lee Rankin the Onyx Ranch and Store, which formerly belonged to William Scodie. This ranch, known for thirty-six years as the Onyx Ranch, had many more old-time cowboys such as Farel Chappell on the payroll, and has a story all its own, too extensive to account for here. Although somewhat modernized, it has retained a lot of the traditions handed down by a century of cattle people.

Who knows, if you drive the dusty road up through Kelso Valley, you might see the ghost of one of the old-time cowboys who helped win the West as he lopes through the sagebrush and cactus, sitting tall and straight in his single-rig saddle on a fiery Coso mustang. And maybe, before your very eyes, a big-eared bull will break out of a clump of willows that border the creek. You may get the chance to see this phantom shake out his reata to rope the bull, throw him, tying him up like a Christmas turkey in jig time. Or if it is just getting dusk you might see the old Landers chuck wagon pulled off on a flat beside the road. As you pause a moment, you can hear the old-time cowpunchers as they sit around the campfire, laughing and talking about some mean horse, a wild bull, or the last night in town. These are truly the unsung heroes of the West, and the nation owes them a debt of gratitude.

Bill Landers has been gone for some time now. But each year for the last fifty, a South Fork eighth grader has gone forward at graduation to accept a scholarship—a scholarship set up for them by the estate of William Landers.

VIII Onyx Store

SETTING back off the road and seeming to fit more into an earlier age looms the Onyx Store. The proprietor of the first store built at Onyx was William Scodie. Born in Prussia in 1827, he learned the art of cooking in Bremen, Germany, as a boy and went to sea as a cook on a merchant ship. His culinary skills then took him to Valparaiso, where he was a hotel cook during the years 1853 and 1854. After a trip to Australia, he came to San Francisco, where he remained until 1856. He then traveled to Keyesville. At that time the only road over Greenhorn Mountain was an ox trail. When he opened a hotel in that mining camp, all his supplies had to be hauled in by pack mules or ox trains. He operated his hotel quite successfully for five years. Then in 1861, he moved to the South Fork and settled at what is now Onyx.

In those days the wagon track the bullwhackers used to take mining supplies from Tulare to the Coso mines did not continue on westward as the highway does today. It turned south just about 100 yards up the road from the present store. After making a jog about 100 yards south and then 300 yards west again, it turned sharply south until it reached the mountain. Then it continued on down the Valley. It was on this old road behind the present store that Scodie built the original store. It, like most of his buildings, was made of native adobe brick.

He lived in the back of this store, and in his front room he began stocking the supplies needed for the cattlemen and miners of the area. This big room had a fireplace which was so large that a horse was required to pull the back logs for the fire up from the river bottom. The logs would then be pushed through the front door and rolled across the dirt floor to the hearth. A homemade table stood in front of his huge fireplace, and Scodie's excellent cooking and cheery welcome soon gained his place a reputation that was hard to equal. Scodie soon became good friends with the Indians, who had a rancheria close by, and finally married one of the young Indian women named White Blanket.

While Scodie was in this first store during 1875, Cleovaro Chavez, who had been a lieutenant for the infamous Tiburcia Vasquez, robbed him of $800, a change of clothes, and horses for him and his gang. After tying up Scodie, they rode off up the Valley to the east.

In 1880 Scodie needed additional room for his expanding business, so he had Captain Andress, who had a ranch several miles up the road, build him the frame building that was still in use in 1970. It was not until 1913, however, that the road was straightened and the store moved to its last location.

In the winter of 1892-93, two fugitives crept up to the door of the store and under cover of darkness, they slipped a grocery list and a $20 gold piece under the door. They then returned to their hiding place at the mouth of Kelso Canyon. These two men were none other than John Sontag and Chris Evans, both of whom had a large price on their heads for train robberies in the Visalia area. They knew it was Scodie's custom to go to the store early in the morning to start the fire and get ready for the day's business. Therefore, they took the chance that he would go along with their plan. The note suggested that Scodie start a man up Kelso Canyon with the groceries, and they would relieve him of them in a way that would not cast suspicion on the storekeeper.

Louie Bowers was working at Onyx at this time and drew the assignment. He was well on his way up Kelso when two masked hombres stepped from behind the cactus and demanded

Scodie's Store, taken in the 1890's. Those identified are: *second from left*, Louie Bowers; *third*, John Landers; *fourth*, W. W. Landers; and *eighth*, William Scodie. *From the right, first*, Hamp Williams Sr.; *fifth*, Gasey Taylor; *sixth*, Jim Mack; *seventh*, Mr. Mills.

that he surrender his load, which they later carried away on their pack horses. When Bowers reported the incident to Scodie, he said they had better not try to make another delivery for a while and hoped they would have better luck next time.

It might seem strange that those two outlaws put their trust in someone they did not know. Scodie could easily have double-crossed them to get the reward the railroad company had placed on their heads. But Sontag and Evans gambled that Scodie would feel, as so many others did, that they had been forced into their life of crime by the Southern Pacific Railroad.

The story has been told that, in the 1870's, in order to help the railroad finance further building, the government had given the company the right to file on every other section along the right-of-way providing it was not already taken. It seems as if too many of these sections already had settlers in the process of proving up on them. The railroad hired gangs of toughs to run out the settlers and thereby leaving the land open for filing. Sontag and Evans were supposed to have been two of those run out. True or not, many people believed this, therefore making it easy for Sontag and Evans to evade the railroad detectives for many years.

Some twenty-five years later Vick Gonzales was working in the hayfields on the Nicoll Ranch with Weaver Hand, and told him the story of how the outlaws got their grocery order. Vick had, in 1900, served time in Folsom Prison for killing an Onyx man. Being a good worker, Vick was put in charge of a road crew and happened to mention the town of Onyx. One of the men, Chris Evans, said that he knew where the town was, and proceeded to tell the account of holding up a delivery man to get the supplies they had already purchased.

In 1903 they had some excitement at the store which caused quite a stir. In the late afternoon Frank Apalatea, Warren Rankin, August Glade and Louie Bowers were in the middle of one of their routine poker games when they heard the clatter of hooves outside. A voice called through the open door, "I want to see the boss man!" Henry Wirth was then leasing the store from Scodie's heirs, and walked to the front where a man sat on a tall bay horse, leading a pack horse, and packing a rifle across his saddle. The man asked where he could get a meal for himself and his horses. Wirth told him to take the horses back to the barn to feed them and, if he would go to the cookhouse, the Chinaman would cook him something to eat. As it was late afternoon, Wirth expected the stranger to stay the night, but about an hour later they again heard horses outside. And again the voice boomed out, "Send out the boss man!" When the storekeeper went to the porch he was greeted by "How much do I owe you?" He was told that it would be fifty cents for his horses and fifty cents for his own meal. To this the traveler looked Henry Wirth in the eye and said "Just charge it to Jim McKinney." When this statement was related inside it caused quite a stir as Jim McKinney was wanted for murder—not only in California, but Arizona as well.

Warren Rankin was at that time constable of Onyx and wanted to take off after McKinney. He had a two-wheeled cart, pulled by two fast horses, and felt he could overtake the outlaw, but the other men talked him into waiting until he obtained more help. Rankin decided that, as it was late, the outlaw would probably sleep in a haystack back off the road. So he phoned Sheriff McCracken in Kernville, and set up a plan to meet early the next morning at the lime dyke on the old Kernville short-cut road.

Warren drove down toward Isabella, cut through the river bottom, and met McCracken. But Jim McKinney was too wary to walk into a trap. Because it was an ideal spot for an ambush he went on foot and led his horse through the rocks north of where the road crossed the dyke. When the two officers realized that their quarry was slipping away, they came into the open and spotted him. After he ignored their repeated shouts to halt, shots were exchanged.

Onyx Store as it appeared in 1970.

Although McKinney managed to make good his escape, he was wounded by one of the shots. It was this wound that led to his being shot down in a Bakersfield joss house, but only after killing Jeff Packard and Will Tibbet, two peace officers.

William Scodie and White Blanket had one daughter named Sophia. When the Post Office Department asked that they choose a new name for the post office, Bill is said to have left it up to his daughter. Scodie, as the settlement had been called, sounded too much like Scotia, a town in northern California. In thumbing through the dictionary, Sophia came across the word "onyx," liked the sound of it, and so named the place. Another likely explanation of the name Onyx was given by Henry Wirth. He said that, in German "onyx" means "old nothing."

After the death of White Blanket, Bill married a woman of German descent and had another daughter, Wilma, who later became Mrs. Ross. William Scodie died in 1898 and the Onyx Store, after being leased by Henry Wirth, Lee Rankin and Phil Glezen—in that order—was finally purchased by Oscar Rudnick and A. J. Alexander. The Rudnick estate, which owned the store in 1970, leased the building to Jess Barr, who was still carrying on the tradition of country storekeeping started by Scodie almost 110 years earlier.

IX More Pioneer Ranches

A MILE down the new road from the Onyx Store is the remains of the Eph Johnson place. Ephraim Johnson was born in Missouri in 1828, and was one of the last of the old bullwhackers. He did teaming with oxen from Santa Fe, New Mexico to El Paso, Texas, then hauled freight in Los Angeles County for four years. Later he located in Glenville where for ten years he hauled from the railhead at Tipton.

It was on one of these trips to Tipton that the following contest took place. It was related as follows many years later by Uncle Jeff Mayfield, then a resident of White River. Eph had come to Tipton with his bull team after a load of freight for White River. While in town waiting for the train he had several drinks, and by the time the freight arrived he was well fortified. When Eph saw the train engine he said, "Huh, that thing can't pull nuthin'; my bull team can pull that thing backwards." After some words were exchanged, the engineer agreed to pull against the ox team. Eph bet his team against the engine on the outcome of the contest.

When everything was ready, and Eph began yelling at his bulls, the engineer put the engine in reverse, and let him think the bulls were beginning to move it. Then he started the engine up, and slowly dragged the bulls backwards a few feet. Eph yelled "wait a minute, I didn't get a good start that time." The next time the engineer pulled the bulls quite a distance, and

Eph had to concede that the engineer had won the bulls. The trainman wouldn't take the oxen, but reports have it that it cost Johnson several hundred dollars in drinks before he was through treating over it.

He also freighted through the South Fork, over Walker Pass to the mines in Inyo County. It was on these trips through the South Fork that Eph spotted the land he wanted, and in 1877 he purchased eighty acres and settled down to a more domestic life. Eph planted a vineyard, an orchard, and a few acres in alfalfa. He soon stopped teaming, but he still loved the rough life connected with it, and would tell of the rough hauls he had made in his younger days whenever he had an audience.

Marvin Powers Sr. with a load of hay for his cattle. He always thought of his stock before himself. Tom and Bess are the team, and the old Powers home is in the background.

Having a vitality that belied his age, he continued to enjoy being out with the fellows. When he was over eighty years, he took a trip with several men from the South Fork to Reno to see the Jeffrey-Johnson fight. Traveling in an early Model T Ford, they paid $20.00 each to see the fight, which lasted only a few minutes. Frank Apalatea, who also went on this jaunt, said Eph was the life of the party, and set a fast pace for his younger companions.

Eph loved to race horses and would bet his "Black Bess" against any in the Valley. On the South Fork the favorite place for these races was on the straight stretch just south of the Hanning Ranch, at the mouth of Kelso Valley. These early contests were also held on Kelly's Ranch, below old Isabella.

Eph had brought to the South Fork his wife, Gelena, five daughters, and a son, who all grew up in the Valley.

Weaver and Hattie Hand on their wedding day.

Mr. and Mrs John Cross, pioneer South Fork settlers.

After Johnson, Clayton Ripley owned the ranch for a while; then in 1919 Marvin Powers, Sr. came out of the Army and bought the old Johnson place. For thirty years he made it the headquarters of his cattle ranch. The old house that Johnson built stood for almost ninety years before it was torn down in 1967. Not only did Marvin Powers, Sr. start his married life in this home, but each of his three sons also started their married lives there. A June apple tree, planted by the old ditch, and a brick storehouse, were all that remained in 1970 to serve as a reminder of Powers' sojourn there.

Marvin's brother, Jack, next owned the ranch, followed by Dr. Sprague, who also owned the next place west along the slope of the mountain, the H. B. True or Kerruish Ranch. Outside of these two ranches the pioneer ranches west of Onyx of Scodie, Curliss, Pruitt, Gibony and Boone have been absorbed by the Rudnick holdings.

47

Weaver Hand got out to open the gate and his wife, Hattie, got out to take his picture. Also shown in the background is their ranch as it appeared in 1920.

As the Kelso Valley Road turns off Highway 178 to the south, it is a nearly impossible task to sort out the individual parcels as they were homesteaded. Yet up this road is a ranch that has been in one family for over fifty years. This is the Weaver Hand Ranch. Weaver was born in White River in 1892 and came to the Valley first in 1915. When he first arrived in the Valley he worked for John Cross on the ranch he purchased four years later.

In reminiscing about his early days in the Valley, Weaver said of Mrs. Cross, "She was a natural born matchmaker and it wasn't long before she had just the girl for me." She planned a party to which most of the young people of the Valley were invited. The girl Mrs. Cross picked for Weaver was Hattie Smith. The two of them hit it off so well that they were soon married. During World War I Weaver joined the Navy. Hattie returned to the Smith Ranch to be with her folks until she could join him later in the Panama Canal Zone. In 1919 he came back to the Valley, bought the Cross Ranch, and he and Hattie moved into the house which in 1970 they were still occupying. In this home eight children were born. All except one were delivered by Dr. W. B. Smith, then of Kernville.

When the Hands moved on the ranch there were only ten acres of cleared land. Weaver soon embarked on a project on which he worked steadily and almost continuously for the next forty years. He had taken out homestead papers on the adjoining 160 acres, and kept acquiring land until, by 1960, he owned over 400 acres. Kelso Creek, where his land is located, contains some of the best soils in the South Fork, as it is made up of layers of accumulated silt, all washed down from the watershed to the south. However, it is not an easy land to level or to maintain in a leveled state, as the waters of Kelso Creek intermittently overflow their banks and cover the crops with from one inch to a foot of mud. Therefore, the same act of nature that makes the land so fertile many times destroys the crops.

The South Fork gets more than its share of wind during certain times of the year, and the fine soil moves with even the slightest breeze. The Joshua Trees posed a problem in land leveling in the horse and mule days and had to be removed. Roots would be dug around as far as possible, then all the roots that could be reached would be cut. Two to four horses were then hooked to the Joshua Tree. The tree would be pulled first one way and then the other, cutting the remaining exposed roots until free. The Joshuas were then dragged into piles to be burned when dried. Leveling followed, and was accomplished with a two- or four-horse Fresno scraper.

All in all, every acre that Weaver put into crops was done the hard way, but he was equal to the task because he was a man of exceptional determination, strength and stamina, coupled with an incessant desire to work. When Weaver finally quit farming, it was not because of health or old age, but as he put it, "the high cost of taxes and the fact that where you used to be able to hire a good man for two dollars a day, it got to where you couldn't hire a poor one for twelve or fourteen dollars." He pointed out that when he quit farming, most of the ranches were supported by some other business.

Weaver's wife, Hattie, was just as small as he was large, weighing less than 100 pounds. This was about 120 less than her husband. Hattie also seemed to have endless energy, and worked long hours with her garden, chickens and milk cows, as well as putting out savory meals for her big family. She also took over as Sunday School Superintendent of the Methodist Church from her mother, Ella P. Smith, and spent many hours doing such jobs as the cleaning of the church, which she did for so many years.

The whole Hand family worked together. The girls, as well as the boys, became accomplished first with horse teams and later with tractors. It was not unusual to see one of the girls driving the teams, hauling 130 pound grain sacks, or irrigating in the fields—which they sometimes preferred to do barefoot. With five daughters in the family, the Hand Ranch was for many years the social center of the Valley. Hattie and Weaver were the gracious hosts to many ice cream socials, hay rides and activities that kids thrive on. The Hand family will not soon be forgotten in the South Fork Valley.

As the highway starts on a straight stretch three miles below Onyx, you can see the buildings of the old Nicoll's Ranch where they stand off to the north side of the road. Bill and John Nicoll came to the Kern River in 1859, where they mined until 1863, when they took up ranches on the South Fork. Bill had his first ranch on Seybert Lane, and the second one on Kelso Creek just above where the Kelso Valley Road first crosses the creek. John Nicoll settled on the property where the buildings are located and in 1891 owned 480 acres. His holdings went as far as the Methodist Church, and the original ranch buildings stood about 200 yards straight behind the church.

John Nicoll was one of the finest of blacksmiths, and when Kern County's first election was held, his blacksmith shop was listed as the polling place for Weldon.

Willie Nicoll ready to leave the home ranch for the high country in the late 1920's. The horse is Peanut, and the mules, *left to right*, are Red and Typo.

Old John Nicoll, pioneer of the South Fork, holds his daughter Alice, and his son Willie stands by his knee. *Standing in rear, left to right*, are his wife Rose and his stepdaughter Bessie Vickers.

In 1884 old John married Miss Elizabeth Carden, and their two children were named Alice and John William, known as Willie. When Elizabeth died, John later married Rose Vickers. Willie, who left home at fourteen to ride for Landers, later took over the old ranch. He ran cattle for years, with a permit for cattle in the high country. Willie is considered to be one of the finest of the old time cowboys. He married Clara Powers, one of Jim Powers' girls, and they raised three boys—Earl, John and Ed, and one girl, Alice.

In 1970 John Nicoll, grandson of Old John, was still on the home ranch where, in connection with his ranch operation, he was still breaking and training young horses. He had a skill acquired not only from a lifetime of being around stock people but also had that gift granted to few—a natural born horseman.

To the south of the ranch, Nicolls Peak looms over the South Fork Valley, named after old John. It is a reminder to the Valley residents of the Nicolls' part in settling the west.

49

X The Church by the Side of the Road

IF ANY one thing could be said to be typical of the South Fork of the Kern River, it would be the Methodist Church at Weldon. Sitting alongside Highway 178, with its backdrop of the Bartolas country, it has served as a true lighthouse to the spiritual, social and cultural life of this mountain community since 1899.

Almost as soon as the first settlers had staked their claims the ministers of the gospel followed. Walking, riding horseback and later using a horse and buggy, they stopped whereever night happened to overtake them. These visits were few and far between in the 1860's, as the closest minister was O. D. Dooley of Glennville. Known better as Parson Dooley, he came over the Greenhorn Mountains to the Kern River whenever he could. In 1866 Parson Dooley had started the Cumberland Presbyterian Church in Glennville, the first church in newly formed Kern County, but he still found time to visit the Kern River area.

In the 1870's a building was erected on the site where the Women's Club hall was later built. This first building was used as the meeting place for the Presbyterian Church in 1873 and also for the Weldon Grange. By the middle of the 1880's this barnlike structure had fallen into sad repair, and finally burned. Services were then held on the second floor of the A. Brown Store at Weldon, or in the schoolhouse.

The neighboring town of Kernville had a larger population and was more centrally located, so became the leader in church activities. One of the leaders in church work from the 1880's to the 1900's was Miss Josie Sumner, who later married a minister by the name of Belknap. Miss Sumner was a teacher in the early Sunday School, played the organ, and many times when there was no minister she

conducted services and held funerals in private homes.

In Kernville, as in most frontier towns, the school building was first used to hold church services. After the Petersen Hall (later the I.O.O.F. Hall) was built, funerals and weddings were held there.

Mrs. Yarborough, then Miss Nettic Hight, gives the following interesting account taken from a letter to her friend, Mrs. Tommy Smith: "In the mining camps such as Keyesville and Greenhorn Mountain, there were one or two old miners who had been taught about the Bible. They worked along at their mines, and on Sunday would put on a 'boiled shirt' and overalls and a little bow tie, walk to some family home and have dinner. Then about 2 P.M. all the miners would doll up in their red and blue flannel shirts and stroll down and listen to the one with the 'boiled shirt' preach. Our home was most often chosen as it was more

Old John Nicoll's grave on the right, in back of the Methodist Church, and above it, Nicoll's Peak, named in his honor. Mr. Nicoll had given the land for the church to be built on, and at his request was buried in the church yard.

central. One fellow who preached was named Walker. He would get so excited he would throw his hands and arms about and stand on his tip-toes as if he were trying to reach Heaven. When there was no-one to preach we children held church and took turns being the preacher."

On November 12, 1870 the Kern River Circuit of the Methodist Church was organized under the Los Angeles District and they held their first quarterly conference in Bakersfield. The Presiding Elder, James Corwin, was the chairman, Lewis R. Reeder was appointed secretary. Present were Edward Tibbit and Phinas Tibbit, but there was no preacher present. In February 1871 the second quarterly conference was also held in Bakersfield, with the same members in attendance with the exception that the Rev. Noah Burton from Visalia also met with them.

No record was made of any more meetings until March 9, 1872, when they again met in the home of Phinas Tibbet in Bakersfield. At this third meeting Jesse L. Bennett was listed as the preacher in charge, and his salary was set at $800 per year. Mention was made that there was a Sabbath School at Bakersfield, with the average attendance of twenty scholars, and that the next quarterly conference was to be held in Tehachapi. However, later records show that it too was held in Bakersfield.

On July 20, 1872, the first meeting of the Kern River Circuit was held on the South Fork and the members met at the Presbyterian Church, which was about a mile west of where the Methodist Church was later built. These meetings all followed the same pattern as the one that

Mrs. Josie "Summer" Belknap, taken in 1905.

Parson Dooley, pioneer minister, and his wife Caroline.

follows: "The Fourth Quarterly Conference for the Kern River Circuit was held at the Cumberland Presbyterian Church on the South Fork of the Kern River. James Corwin P. E. in the chair. Conference was opened by prayer by the P. E.

Members present:
Jesse L. Bennett, Preacher in Charge.
W. J. Grant, Chap. Leader.
Thos. H. Smith, Steward.

1. Are there any complaints? Answer: No.
2. Are there any appeals? Answer: No.
3. Is there any report from the pastor? Answer: See report.
4. What has been raised during the Quarter for the support of the ministry and how has it been applied: Answer:

South Fork $18.00
Tehachapi 4.00
Walker's Basin 5.00
Bakersfield 66.00
Applied on Preacher's Salary . . . 66.50
Missionary appropriation 25.00
_____
$91.00

Father Bennett. Taken in 1868.

5. Phinas Tibbit, Lewis Reeder, Edward Tibbit, T. H. Smith and W. J. Grant were elected Stewards. T. H. Smith was elected Recording Steward.

6. Will you now attend to the examination of character? The name of J. L. Bennett was called. Character examined and passed.

7. Have the General Rules been read this Quarter? Answer: No.

Is there any other business? Answer: No.

Where shall the next Quarterly Meeting be held? Answer: at Bakersfield.

Minutes read and approved. Signed: James Corwin, P. E. and W. J. Grant, Secretary.

Jesse L. Bennett, known affectionately to those who lived in the mountain region as Father Bennett, was born in the State of Virginia in 1810. Heralded as the Father of Methodism, he moved to Nevada in 1849. He preached at Genoa and Eagle Ranch, which is now Carson City. In 1860 he also conducted services in Virginia City where, for lack of a church he preached in a bar, cleaned out for the occasion by the bartender. Father Bennett later recounted that he was overcome by the amount of gold and silver donated when he passed his hat, not realizing that the miners appreciated the music, singing and preaching with equal zest. He often held burial services and weddings in bars also. In 1869 Bennett was appointed to the San Bernardino Circuit which was later changed to the Anaheim Circuit. This circuit was very poor, and as Father Bennett

had no horse, he had to travel on foot to get to his new appointment in El Monte.

A short time later he was employed to travel the Kern River Circuit. With only $100 in missionary money, he left his family in Anaheim and set out on horseback to his new circuit. With the little money he had and with the help of some friends, a few months later he was able to move his family to the South Fork of the Kern River. Besides his wife, the family consisted of one son, Charles, and three daughters—Annie, Edith (later Mrs. Charlie Taylor) and Nellie.

In reminiscing about this man of God, Nettie Hight Yarborough recounted the following: "He walked over to Tehachapi from Kernville when Mother was teaching there. She gave him $2.50 to pay his way home, but he refused to use it in this manner. He wanted to take it to his family, so he walked all the way back home." Many South Fork couples started married life with Jesse L. Bennett reading the wedding vows. In the mid-1870's the people of the circuit gave Father Bennett a piece of land in Kernville and built a house on it for him. Here he lived and preached until his death in 1886.

In 1886, while Rev. W. S. Clinesmith was pastor, a person came to the South Fork who left a lasting impression on the hearts and minds of those who lived there. This was Ella P. Meriam, later Mrs. Tommy Smith. Mrs. Smith, known to most as Grandmother Smith, came to the Valley as a school teacher. She taught at the Scodie School, which was a quarter of a mile east of the Smith Ranch. Mrs. Charlotte Pettypool wrote the following tribute to Mrs. Smith:

"She was my school teacher when I was very young and also my Sunday School teacher. She was the only teacher I ever had who opened school each morning with prayers and the singing of hymns. After her marriage to 'Tommy' Smith, she organized the King's Daughters and Sons Society in her home where all the pupils of her earlier teaching met weekly to receive spiritual and domestic training. We girls learned to sew and the boys were instructed in the art of sewing on buttons." It was at one of these meetings that Grandmother Smith reported the following: "The girls were to tell at each meeting what they had done for Jesus. One small girl said at one meeting, 'I helped a little chicken find its mama.' "

Grandmother Smith was just twenty-one when she came to the Valley. After helping start the Sunday School for the Methodist Church in 1886, she taught there for 67 years. Sixty of these years she served as superintendent of the Church School. Through the years Grandmother Smith gave out Sunday School papers to a large number of children outside the church. In this way her influence extended in a very real way throughout the community.

Her son-in-law, Weaver Hand, wrote the following while she was still living: "Grandmother is just the best mother-in-law a fellow ever had. Gentle, kind and wise. A fellow must try to make good because she knows you can and she expects you to."

So many of the things Grandmother Smith did for the people of the Valley seem too small to mention. But it was these same small deeds, performed over so many years out of a loving heart, that so endeared her to all who knew her.

Rev. J. C. Livingston, who was preaching at the Weldon Church in 1899, will not soon be forgotten by Valley residents. Mrs. Lottie Pettypool recounts the following about him, and the building of the churches at Weldon, Kernville and Isabella. "The thing that I think endeared Mr. Livingston to us was his steadfast, unfailing faith even under the most adverse circumstances. In the building of the churches, he labored under the most trying, discouraging difficulties. The church membership was small and we were perfect 'Doubting Thomases' when the idea of even building one church was presented to us. 'It can't be done' we said. But with a gentle, kindly smile lighting his face, Livingston said with characteristic confidence, 'We will build the churches by faith—all three of them.' And that is exactly how they were built. One was built in Kernville in 1898, one at Weldon in 1899, and another in Isabella in 1904. Rev. Livingston preached that 'Faith without works is dead' and he was on the job whenever possible."

Livingston was a wheelwright by trade before entering the ministry, so he was handy with tools. He was personally helped on the job by many, but one who put in more hours than most

Grandmother Smith. She "lived the faith."

was a carpenter by the name of Ed Darling. He helped put up the framework of the Weldon Church. When the framework and siding were almost completed, the church was blown over, with Rev. Livingston and Charles Likely inside. With the jack-screws, timbers and community help, the building was put back on its foundation and finished enough to hold dedication services. Lumber was contracted from Brown's Mill on Greenhorn, and the flooring, casings, rustic, and ceilings were made by Mr. Likely at the same mill. Ed Pettypool also worked many hours in construction, helping install the siding and flooring.

In those days the minister was furnished with a horse or mule and a buggy to cover his circuit. Hardly ever was this a fancy high-stepping filly. More often they were just old plugs. Some of the early church members said they thought this could have been a blessing in disguise, as the minister's constant activity to coax the horse into a lazy trot might have been that which kept him from freezing to death on the long circuit trips in the open buggy.

53

Rev. J. C. Livingston and daughter.

Ministers had to ford the river coming from Kernville. The ford most used was Tilley Crossing, located at the confluence of Tilley Creek and the Kern. Rev. Burton Hamlin, who was the minister in 1908, always depended on his notes. You can imagine his despair when he discovered these were lost when he encountered difficulty in fording Tilley Crossing during high flow.

These early ministers were usually welcome whenever they stopped. Certain places, though, were more common stops for dinner and overnight stays. On the South Fork, some of these were the homes of J. B. Batz, Bob Neil, H. B. True, E. A. Johnson and T. H. Smith.

The Batz family lived on the old Kissack Ranch in the 1880's. One evening Mrs. Batz saw the preacher coming down the road and, being very busy, made some remark about visitors, but did not notice her young daughter by her side. She went into the house to make herself presentable, and was mortified to overhear little Daisy say "Mamma says she wishes you wouldn't come here so often."

54

Rev. Hamlin seemed to consider that the hardest thing he had to deal with on the charge were the twelve church lamps. These had to be filled with coal oil, wicks trimmed, and chimneys polished. Custodians were unheard of in those days.

Many times the ministers' salaries were supplemented with money raised by an ice cream social. These get-togethers were usually held at the end of each church year at Bob Neil's home and made about $50. Obtaining the required ice was a major chore. Word was sent to John Neil at Hot Springs (Scovern) who then would ship the ice up on horsedrawn stage the day before it was to be used. Plenty of blankets and quilts were sent down with the order—which was much greater than they actually needed—to allow for melting. A quartet of children often sang for these socials. They were Kinnie Powers, Laurie Rankin, Ettie Powers, and Helen Smith, ages eight to eleven, with Hattie Smith as organist.

Much of the ministers' subsistence came from what people gave them and what they gathered off the land. Rev. A. D. Willett, Pastor in 1919, gave the following account of how he got meat for the week. "Monday—shoot a jack; Wednesday—get some trout; Friday—some eggs from Bob Neil; Saturday—a chunk of beef from the butchering at Onyx."

People seemed to have more time for the spiritual things of life, and Sunday was set aside totally for religion. People such as the Kissacks, who lived 7½ miles from the church, spent three to four hours each Sunday in travel. In summer the Smith children got very thirsty

Andress and Pettypool families on their way to church

Smith's first car.

Some of the mainstays of the Methodist Church at Weldon: *left to right*, Lottie Pettypool, Helen Alexander, Nellie Milligan, her daughter Harriet, Mrs. Phil Hand, Miss Millie Neill, and Ella Smith.

riding to church in their spring wagon drawn by two mules, so they took bottles of water and a sack of apples to eat on the way home.

The coming of the automobile cut down traveling time. The auto was a hard thing, though, for many of the old timers to adjust to. Grandfather Smith was one of these who had a hard time adjusting. The first time he could be induced to go for a ride was coming home from church. He sat in stony silence for the whole four miles, and when they pulled into the Smith yard, Mr. Smith threw his arms up in the air

Group of old timers at Weldon Methodist Church. *Back row, left to right*, Jim Kissack, Ed Kewin, Mr. Ashby (minister), Weaver Hand, Bill Kissack Sr., Granddad Alexander, Art Alexander, Bob Neill. *Middle row, left to right*, Chuck Phillips, Earl Phillips, unidentified, Miss Millie Neill, unidentified, Bill Kissack Jr., Jessie Kissack, Ella Smith, Hattie Hand, Jessie Phillips, and behind her, Ruth Potter, Bert James, Bob Tracy. *Seated, back row*, Clara Nicoll. *Seated front row, left to right*, Francis Hand, Dorothy Hand, Bernice Phillips, Eleanor Potter, *and last*, Mrs. Bert James.

and dramatically exclaimed, "Praise the Lord for a safe journey home," seriously meaning every word.

To the South Fork Valley came people from many parts of the United States, Canada, Scotland, and the Isle of Man. Those best remembered from the latter were the Kissacks. Bill Sr. and Jessie were a great credit to the community as well as the church. Jessie could be seen in her gum rubber boots shoveling ditch right along with the menfolk, or taking care of her turkeys in the morning and evening. On Sunday, though, she and her family could always be found in church. She often sang in her sweet brogue and was accompanied by her son, Jim, who had a voice without equal in the Valley.

Bob Neil, also from the Isle of Man, was said to have lived a life of kindness to every living creature. He and his sister, Millie, loved all the children of the Valley and quite often fed the ministers Sunday dinner. The William Joughin family, the Pettypools, A. J. Alexanders, Phil and Edith Hand, and, of course, the Thomas H. Smith family, his daughter-in-law, Ella, and her daughter, Hattie, and others too numerous to mention have made the Weldon Methodist Church a true lighthouse in the spiritual, social and cultural life of this mountain community.

XI Seybert Lane

ALMOST a mile down the highway from the church, Fay Ranch Road turns north. This pioneer road was first called Martin Lane, and later Seybert Lane, after early families who settled along its cottonwood shaded boundaries. Across the highway to the south you can see the foundation of the old South Fork Women's Club hall. This club, originally called the South Fork Recreation Club, was formed on May 11, 1914 and has been extremely active through the years. Its founders were Mesdames Tommy Smith, Lee Rankin and Warren Rankin. Almost as soon as the club was formed they started raising money to build a hall at Weldon. This they did by sponsoring a series of dances which alternated between Lee Rankin's cook house at Onyx (which stood just north of the old Onyx Store), the top floor of the A. Brown Store at Weldon, and the old adobe hall in Isabella, built by John Hooper. These events, in most cases, lasted all night, and the women would bring their specialties for a midnight meal.

When meeting in the old adobe hall at Isabella there was no cook house handy from which to borrow table service, so the A. Brown Company at Kernville took dishes off their shelves. After the dance was over they were washed and returned to the shelves. The A. Brown Company didn't discount these items, but they didn't charge any extra after they had been broken in—so nobody complained.

After more than a year's hard work enough money was raised to build the hall. The first hall stood just across Highway 178 from the store and school, and before it was completed dances were being held. Those at the dance, though, admitted that everyone had to dance in order to keep warm, as it was still winter time.

As you entered this old hall there was a cloak room on the right, with two small double bunks built into one corner. This was before the days of baby sitters, and the whole family went to everything together. When it was feeding time for one of the little ones, the mother would go into the cloak room to let the baby nurse. In short order she was back dancing the Paul Jones. There were no bars within five miles, but every now and then a few of the men would go out for "a breath of fresh air" and would come back in completely refreshed, swinging the gals even higher than usual.

It was a sad moment for the Valley when one night, in 1949, this building caught fire and burned. But with the usual industry, another building was standing by 1952 on land donated by Jim and Ann Robertson. This building can be seen on the right as you start up the lane. Early in the 1900's the Robertsons had pushed their daughter, Evelyn, to the dances in her big buggy so she could use it for a bed in case the bunks were all full.

There has been a country store on the east corner of the lane since 1927, when the first one was built and operated by Walter Alexander. This crossroads store was later run by L. S. Diamond, Earl Gordon, Paul Rhoads and Deak Leazenby, in that order. Leazenby, who rented the store in 1948, was still operating it in 1970.

Although many have passed through the door of the little country store, there are none who held better memories of it than the children who filed across the road from the school over the years to spend their pennies and nickels. It took considerable time out of what was often the busiest part of the day to wait on the school children who shopped with such diligence, but there was never a complaint from the harried storekeeper. In later years the school board made a ruling that proved very profitable for the cough drop companies. This was that the children would only be able to leave the school yard and go to the store for cough drops and

South Fork Women's Club group about 1916. Standing on the porch of the Batz house, *from right to left*, Mrs. Boone, Eva Powers, Mrs. Warren Rankin, Dorothy Anderson, Virginia Williams, Betty Powers, Ella Smith, Ann Robertson holding Bernice Phillips, Mrs. Ethel Joughin, in front of her, Maud Walton, on the left of the step, *left to right*, Helen Smith, Mrs. Cleo Cross holding daughter Helen, Evelyn Powers, Mrs. John Hooper, Mary Rankin holding daughter Alice, Mrs. Lee Rankin holding son Leroy, with son Billy below her.

other medical supplies, and then only with a note from their parents. Although the South Fork is normally considered to have a very healthy climate, coughs seemed to persist, and cough drops continued to be a best seller.

The first school had been built in the west end of this school yard in 1873 and some of the families such as the Alexanders and Nicolls, have had three generations of attendance at the same school. One of the best remembered teachers from the 1800's was Emma Johnson, daughter of Eph Johnson of Onyx. Others who taught at the Weldon School for many years were Mrs. Garroutte and Mrs. C. E. Jones. The Valley residents used to say that the only way they ever got any new blood in the Valley was by one of the local boys marrying one of the school teachers. A few cases where this happened are listed

by the married names of the teachers: Mrs. Tommy Smith, Mrs. Stanley Smith, Mrs. Bert James, Mrs. John Nicoll, Mrs. Jim Alexander, and Mrs. Bill Kissack.

Many tales have been handed down about the pranks pulled by some of the older boys. One concerned the night in the early 1900's when the bell was stolen from the top of the

South Fork Women's Club Hall when it was being built in 1916.

Weldon School, 1894. *Standing, left to right,* Domingues Bencoma, Teacher Emma Johnson, Bert DeWitt, Oscar Couch, Laura Bencoma, Ida Thurston, Chris Wirth, Harry Fugitt, Pearl Johnson, Edith Fugitt, Pearl DeWitt, Carl Gibony, and Ramon Bencoma. *Middle row,* Grace Thurston, Annie Alexander, Dora DeWitt; *last girl standing,* Grace Gibony. *Front row,* Bernie Couch, Walter Gibony, Louis Couch, Ora Titcomb.

school building. The boys managed to get it to the ground but found it was a lot heavier than they expected. Realizing the consequences if they were discovered in the act, they were prompted to bury the bell. In the 1960's some of the children digging in the school yard uncovered it. Rumors flew of the names of those involved but, on the whole, mystery still surrounds the act. One thing is certain—the community was so overjoyed to get the bell back they had it made into a monument in the front of the school yard.

One prank that was quite expensive occurred when some boys dropped a stick of stove wood into the well casing, making it necessary to drill a new well. Another activity reported to have kept the teachers on their toes was tossing a handful of rifle or shotgun shells into the big wood heater in the back of the school room.

In 1921 more room was needed, so the little one-room school house from the McCray Ranch, formerly called the South Fork School, was moved up and placed beside the first school. The next year the brick building was started on the east end of the school grounds, and this building was used until 1953 when it was condemned because of earthquake damage.

Transportation to and from school has changed immensely since the days the Palmer children rode their burros to school from the Palmer Ranch on the north end of Seybert Lane. Even the first motorized school bus, which was an old Reo truck with no cab, and benches built in back for the children to sit on, was a far cry

Weldon School—1920. Children are, *left to right, back row,* Charles Boone, Earl Nicoll, Mabel Alexander, Virginia Palmer, Mildred Short, Beatrice Jenkins, Miss Eaton (teacher); *second row,* Alice Alexander, Virginia O'Tea, Catilda O'Tea, Evelyn Palmer, Kathryn Laury; *front row,* John Nicoll, Joe Laury, Eddie Nicoll, John O'Tea, unidentified, Grace Miranda, Angela Laury, Shirley Andress, Mike O'Tea, Salvadore Gomez, Pete Miranda. The next year the name was changed to South Fork School.

First School at Weldon, built in 1873.

from the big, modern buses used in the 1970's. One of the best remembered of the bus drivers of the old days was John Miles. In 1970 the principal of the South Fork School was Mrs. Winifred Henderson, who had attended that school for eight years of grammar school. Her great-grandfather was Thomas H. Smith and her grandchildren make the seventh generation to have lived in the Valley. The school custodian in that same year was Marvin Powers, Jr., an employee of the school district for many years. Marvin had lived on the South Fork all his life and attended grammar school there. His wife, Leah, also was a cook in the school cafeteria for many years. Marvin was also a great-grandson of Thomas H. Smith.

Robert Seybert could often be seen walking down the lane with his old muzzle loading rifle, which was his consant companion.

A mile and three-tenths on up the lane was the home of Robert Seybert, who came to the Valley in 1885. He bought the ranch of B. Martin—later to be his son-in-law. Some of the old buildings were still standing on the west side of the lane in 1970.

Robert had come west in 1849, but barely made the journey. His father, Peter Seybert, was killed in a skirmish when their wagon train ran into a band of hostile Indians. Although Robert was captured, he later managed to escape, and settled in the Los Angeles area. His wife, called "Mary" by the Valley residents, was the former Antonio Maria Soto, grand-daughter of Don José Saturino Moreno—one of the first eleven settlers to bring their families in 1781 into what is now Los Angeles. Don Saturino Moreno and his wife, Dona Maria Guadalupe Gaspar, were both natives of the colonial mining town of El Real Del Rosario. This was in the province of Sinaloa, Nueva España or New Spain—as Mexico was called in colonial times. The Morenos' lot, which was given them by the Spanish government, was located approximately where Sunset and North Broadway join today. This settlement was known as "El Pueblo de Nuestra Señora la Reina de Los Angeles" or Pueblo of our Lady the Queen of the Angels.

Robert and Mary were married at Mission San Luis Rey and lived for a while in San Diego, where their seven children were born. Later they moved to San Bernardino where their daughter, Guadalupe, married Daniel Thomas in 1875. Lupe and Daniel were the parents of five children: Sarah, Ida, Druzella, Robert and Monroe. When the Seyberts came to the South Fork of the Kern in 1885, the Thomases also came along. In 1886 Daniel died while working on the Fay Ranch. In 1890 Lupe married Henry R. Chrysler and they added another five children to their family. These were Neva, Frank, Frieda, Agnes and Joseph.

When the Seyberts came to the Valley they brought with them five daughters, who eventually married Valley men. Alice married B. Martin, who was at that time a hog man for A. Brown Company. After he died, she married Jack Fletcher, a pioneer Valley blacksmith and also one of the first forest rangers. Joaquina married John DeWitt. Cynthia married Bob Pruitt, who later worked for the Kern County Sheriff Department. Victoria entered into wedlock with Johnny Johnson. The youngest daughter, Mary, was a dwarf. Mary put an ad in one of the lonely heart columns of the day, and Alex Sellars answered the inquiry. He came to the South Fork and took Mary for his bride. For many years Alex held the job of stud horse man for the A. Brown Company. The youngest of the Seybert family was Philip. Philip's life ran the normal course of so many of the South Fork young men. This included working as a cowboy for the A. Brown Company, and cooking for the Landers chuck wagon. The work was not the safest in the world, and Phil had his right eye knocked out when a mean horse threw its head up just as Seybert was leaning forward to dismount.

Most of Phil's leisure hours were spent with the young men of the Valley as they rode to visit neighboring towns. It was one of these trips that brought Seybert's life to a violent end at the age of thirty. The report of this death can be found in the September 26, Vol. 8, issue of the *Daily Californian*, printed in Bakersfield in 1895.

It seems that young Seybert had gone to Kernville for a whirl in the Chinese gambling houses with a few friends. Among these were Pat Vega and John Weldon. While there, they were having a few drinks with Gabe Chavez, when they met some Indians from the South Fork. The Indians were listed as Pablo, Louie, and Indian Willie—also known as Willie Archer. Phil became involved in an argument with Indian Willie, who was at that time riding for the Landers Cattle Company, about the quality of the food served on the Landers wagon, and as Phil was walking away, Willie, evidently wanting the last word, fired two shots from a pistol into Seybert's back. The wounds were such that he died within a few hours.

Constable Clark arrested Indian Willie and put him in the Kernville jail. A coroner's jury the next morning returned the verdict that Seybert came to his death from a shot fired with criminal intent by Indian Willie. The details of what happened during the next twenty-four hours are sketchy, and even the reporter who wrote the news item in 1895 admitted that it took "considerable reading between the lines to get at the exact facts of the case." Even the headlines on the news item were strange, as they proclaimed "A Double Tragedy—Murder and Lynching at Kernville; Philip Seybert killed on Sunday and Willie Archer, his murderer, shot and cut to death on Monday."

Although lynching is not mentioned again, there must have been talk of such actions that prompted Constable Clark to move the prisoner to—as he put it—"a safer place." For on the evening of the day following Seybert's death, he went down to the jail. After taking the prisoner out and locking the door, he turned back, only to be confronted by Robert Seybert — father of the murdered man. A shot was fired and Willie cried out, then ran down the street. The newspaper reported that there followed a fusillade of shots and that the constable, being

Druzilla Thomas and Mary Seybert.

unarmed, did not pursue the investigation. It seems odd that the constable would go about such a chore without being armed, but it appears he did.

When Indian Willie was taken from the street, he had no less than six bullet holes in different parts of his body, three knife cuts on his head, and one on his wrist. Dr. Cash, who attended him, said that any five of the six bullet wounds would have been fatal, but his vitality was such that he did not die for some five hours.

At the inquest into Willie's death, Constable Charles A. Clark was the first witness, and his testimony in part follows:

"I brought him out of the jail and as I was locking the door I saw Mr. Seybert a few feet in front of the jail and he fired a shot, I think from a pistol. The deceased uttered an exclamation and started to run. I caught hold of Seybert but he broke away and started after the deceased. I followed and there was another shot, then I stopped as I had no arms."

Clark further testified that he "saw no other parties near enough to recognize them;" that he heard other shots but "could not tell who fired them." He was asked if he knew if Sey-

Charlie and Etta Andress on their wedding day.

bert shot at the deceased and answered, "I might be mistaken, it was very dark."

Dr. Cash also testified that all the wounds were caused from guns of different calibre. Roswell G. Tibbits, owner of the American Eagle Hotel, swore that he heard the seven shots and they were apparently from pistols of different calibre.

The jury returned the verdict that, "the deceased was Willie Archer and that he had come to his death from gunshot wounds; the wounds were caused by parties unknown to this jury." One of the members of the coroner's jury was Sam Gann, who only three years before had been with Johnny Powers and Oliver McCoy when they were killed by Indians at Sage Canyon. Possibly his findings on this jury could have been influenced by this prior event.

One account relates that Indian Willie was put before a firing squad, and the bullet believed to have ended his life may have come from the gun of Seybert's father. Instead of a

firing squad theory, it possibly was more likened to a shooting gallery, with Indian Willie the target as he dashed like a frightened rabbit through the streets of Kernville.

The next morning Old Sibe, as Seybert was called, was back at his job feeding cottonwood logs into the firebox of the mill boiler at the A. Brown flour mill. Some of the old-timers say that in later years Old Sibe would edge up beside them and state, "I killed me an Injin when the sun was just this high," indicating the sun was about ready to go down. Then he would nudge them in the ribs to show he intended them to laugh with him.

The Seybert Ranch was known for years as the Andress Ranch. Charlie Andress, son of Captain Andress, and his wife, Etta, raised their two daughters, Shirley and Carrie, while they used this old ranch as the headquarters for their cattle operation. Charlie had his cow camp at the north end of Big Meadow in the high country, and it was a popular spot with anyone who happened to be in that part of the plateau. They were assured of a hearty welcome and a good meal, which usually included some homemade bread made in a Dutch oven by Charlie's brother Ernie.

Also established along Seybert Lane were the pioneer ranches belonging to Ramon Bencoma, Bill Nicoll and Johnny Powers. After Johnny's death in 1891, Morge Wallace owned this ranch, and in 1901 Add Cross made this his home.

A group of old time cowboys at Andress Camp at Big Meadow. *Left*, Johnny Johnson, Chris Wirth, Ramon Bencoma, Ernest Andress, Mr. Trawver, and Charlie Andress.

Later it was better known as the Palmer Place, after Robert Palmer moved there with his family. Robert's son, Buzz, quit the ranching business to go into the horse shoeing trade in the Hanford area, and soon gained a reputation as being one of the best in the trade.

John Tilley was one of the first settlers on this Lane north of the river in 1861, but after he was washed out in the flood of 1862 he moved over to the Kernville area. Tilley also later owned the Fay Ranch, located at the end of this road, some seven miles from Highway 178.

As you continue to climb for the last five miles you enter a different world. First to catch your eye are the rolling meadows, set like jewels with their borders of chaparral and bull pine.

Alvin Fay, who was County Supervisor for the first district in 1880 and a well known County surveyor, settled on the original 360 acres. He soon lost it, though, to John Tilley for an $800 mortgage. It was passed down to John's daughter, Carrie, and in 1914 she and her husband, Newell Beaty, moved here with their family consisting of two sons, Bill and Pem, and a daughter, Zora. Carrie and Newell made it their home for twenty-one years. Newell's father, John Beaty, had lived on the South Fork off and on since 1874 and had homesteaded the Hillside Ranch. John was known as the champion hog caller of the South Fork Valley, and from the A. Brown headquarters could call hogs clear from the Murphy Ranch some five miles west. In later years John spent quite a bit of time with his son on the Fay Ranch. The Beaty family filed on more land, and acquired a permit in the high country, and packed people into the mountains for fishing and hunting trips. Another project the Beatys initiated was to pipe water from Fay Creek to power a generator that furnished electricity for the ranch.

The Beatys at the Fay Ranch. *Left to right*, Newell, Carrie, Zora, Pem and Grandfather John Beaty.

Beaty Family. *Left*, Carrie, Zora, Bill, Pem and Newell. Taken about 1918.

In 1935 the Beatys sold the ranch to Jack Crawford and Cyrus Bell. When Crawford and Bell bought the ranch the only buildings were a small adobe dwelling the Beatys had built, and several small sheds and outbuildings. Immediately a building program started which lasted over a year. In 1935 there were few craftsmen in the Valley, so a crew of 35 carpenters and other tradesmen were brought up from the Southland. A commissary was set up, and presided over by Mrs. Lee. On an oak-covered knoll, overlooking the South Fork Valley, three beautiful homes were built.

The most impressive home was that of Jack Crawford which some 35 years later was still considered one of the finest in the Valley. Buzz Palmer, one of the local ranchers, brought his team up and did the clearing and filling. The southwest side of the Crawford home required fourteen feet of footing, and soil was brought in by a horse-drawn Fresno scraper. Palmer received $8.00 a day for his efforts. This was considered a lot of money in those days.

After Palmer finished his dirt moving work on the Fay Ranch he was hired by the Rexroths, the contractors who had just completed the new bridge over the South Fork, to move fill in both ends of the bridge. The building program on the ranch also included the building of a barn and additional sheds.

Taylor Meadow, in the high country, was purchased from Sumner Brown in 1936 and a cabin was also constructed there. It was during the building of this cabin that John, Jack Crawford's son, had an experience that he never forgot. Sleeping a little late one morning, he was awakened by the command, "don't move, don't move." The voice was that of Bert Davis who had spied a huge rattlesnake crawling up on John's bed to catch the warming rays of the morning sun. Davis explained the situation to young Crawford and said he would remedy it. A shotgun was close by, so by lying close to the ground and firing at point blank range, Davis blasted the rattler into oblivion without as much as cutting a thread on the bed canvas. Needless to say, Crawford's nerves were none too steady the rest of the day.

In the 1960's Jack Crawford sold his interest in the ranch to Dr. Ashley, but he and his son kept their homes there, and in 1970 John and his wife Alice continued to make Fay Ranch their home.

Robert "Buz" Palmer, pioneer South Fork blacksmith and horse shoer, taken in the 1960's.

XII Cattle on the Open Range

JUST west of the Weldon School stood the home of the late William Alexander, known to the Valley residents as Bill Aleck. Remembered most for his dry humor and easy going ways, he made friends wherever he went. Bill was only eight months old when his parents, David and Rebecca Alexander, brought him to the South Fork from Scotland.

He started working on the various ranches and by the time he was seventeen he was driving freight teams for the A. Brown Company at Weldon. Hauling from the ranch to the railhead at Caliente, his loads consisted of hogs fattened on the ranch and flour milled at Weldon. On the return trip he hauled everything from supplies for the A. Brown stores at Havilah, Kernville, and Weldon, to heavy equipment for the Kern River Power Company. His teaming jobs also included hauling lumber down the steep and narrow roads from the A. Brown mill on Greenhorn Mountain through Wagy Flat to Kernville.

An account related by Bill's sister, Ann, gives some idea of the hours these teamsters kept. Ann stated that many times she would run ahead of the wagons with a lantern early in the morning, opening the gates on the ranch for the teamsters. It was after one of these early starts that the following incident occurred. The men had stopped the wagons on the road to rearrange the load just before reaching the lower Rankin Ranch, now located just off the rocky point at the west end of Kissack Cove. In doing so, some grain trickled to the ground. Almost immediately three chickens jumped down from the running gear of the wagon for their morning feed. They had roosted there the night before and the men had left the ranch before the chickens were up, which is pretty early.

In 1913, Bill and his brother-in-law, Jim Robertson, bought the Wirth Ranch at Weldon, which they later divided into two separate ranches. In 1920, Bill married Dorothy Anderson and they worked the ranch together. When

Bill and Dorothy Alexander taken in 1920.

Marvin Sr. and Isabel Powers. Taken in 1919 on their wedding day.

the children, Lois and Keith, came along they, too, helped on the ranch. Bill was active in the Kern County Cattlemen's Association and in 1961 was named "Cattleman of the Year" for this organization. In 1970, Keith was running the ranch as his father did until his death in 1965.

Jim Robertson's place is just west of Alexander's. Jim and his wife, Ann, moved into the old Wirth house, built in 1875. They raised their daughter, Evelyn, in a setting that helped her to have the same love for the cattle business that her parents had. She soon became a top hand and was able to handle any ranch job that came her way. After Jim's retirement, he and Ann built a new home closer to the highway, and here they enjoyed the company of many friends who came to visit.

Alexander and Robertson depended on public grazing lands to sustain their herds during most of the year. For the better part of thirty years their cattle operation brought them into close contact with two other cattlemen. These

were Marvin P. Powers and Stanley L. Smith.

Marvin was born at Onyx in 1894. Not unusual for that time and place, he learned to ride horseback almost as soon as he learned to walk. Working cattle became second nature to Marvin. By the time he was fifteen, he was employed as a cowhand for the A. Brown Company of Weldon. He continued to work cattle on various ranches until joining the Army during World War I. He was discharged in 1919 and, in that year, he married Isabell Anderson, sister of Mrs. William Alexander. This was also the year he obtained his first grazing permit in the high country. Marvin loved every foot of the many acres on which he ran cattle, and his love for the open range was second only to his feeling for livestock.

Marvin and Isabell raised their sons, Marvin W., Robert L., and William K., in an environment of which many children would be envious.

Bill Alexander with jerkline team, hauling to A. Brown Store at Kernville.

Jim and Ann Robertson on their wedding day.

With the hard work expected of young people who lived on a ranch, there also came many good times. Most of those best remembered were in connection with time spent in the high country on the summer range. All three boys went into the mountains at an early age. Bob started the youngest. He was only a year old when he rode horseback the fifty miles from the ranch to the mountains on a pillow in front of his father. The Powers boys learned the cattle operation at an early age, and all enjoyed that type of life.

The other member of the cattlemen's quartet was Stanley Smith. In 1895, Stanley was born in the Cottage Grove home on the Smith Ranch at Onyx. Cottage Grove was built by Smith's and Powers' grandfather, Thomas Hooper

Smith, in 1862. When Stanley married Gwen Bruns, in 1928, they moved into the old house, and in 1970 they were still residing there. After two daughters, Joyce and Loraine, were born into the family, they grew up in the ranching tradition by working cattle whenever their help was required. After Joyce became Mrs. Buzz Shaw, she and her husband lived on the eastern portion of the Smith Ranch. They ran their cattle with Stanley's, helping with all ranch work.

Early in the Alexander-Robertson-Powers-Smith association, it became apparent that Stanley Smith had the rare ability to manage men tactfully, patiently, and firmly. It was agreed among the other three that Stanley should be rodeo boss of the cattle operation. So appointed, he began this position in 1920. The rodeo boss had the final say-so regarding cattle on the summer range and the drives to and from the range. A certain amount of discussion was allowed concerning how and when to work the cattle, but the daily plan of work and the final decisions were the responsibility of the rodeo boss. Stanley Smith handled the job ably.

Few changes in operation methods have been made over the years. Few were necessary. The early settlers who followed the Indian trails into the mountain meadows soon learned the secrets of making the most of their range land. This hard-earned knowledge has been passed down from generation to generation.

Formation of the Forest Service in the early 1900's curtailed to some degree the freedom on grazing land. Each cattle operation may vary slightly, depending upon the location of the home ranch, type of range, and time of year that

Stanley and Gwen Smith—1968.

feed is available at any given site. The overall pattern and routine remained fairly constant.

The following account dealing with these four cattlemen, who for over a quarter of a century ran cattle jointly on the Fish Creek allotment, is given with the hope that it may furnish some insight into the great cattle industry and lives of families associated with it.

A cattleman's life is a series of predetermined annual events. Possibly breaking the yearly cycle in November, when the dry cattle (this means there are no cows with calves still nursing) are turned out on the winter range, is as good a place as any to begin.

The four Fish Creek cattlemen ran cow and calf outfits. This means that the cow herd was maintained year after year with only the bulk of the annual calf crop and old cows no longer producing calves being sold. These were replaced by heifers from the calf crop so that the breeding herd was kept at the desired number.

Calves were usually born from the first of March through the month of May on the winter and spring range. At about eight months of age they were weaned and kept on the ranch for three or four months. There they were fed hay and feed supplement, such as cottonseed cake. The calves were sold sometime after the first of the year when people became tired of eating turkey and the beef market correspondingly improved. Always a certain number of cows with calves too small to wean were kept on the ranch and fed hay through the winter. The bulls were also kept on the ranch in the winter, and were not turned out with the cow herd until the latter part of June.

With this background, the cycle begins from when the calves have been taken from the cows and it is time to drive the dry cows to the winter range. The winter range is all government-owned land. Qualified cattlemen are issued grazing permits by the Bureau of Land Management. These permits entitle the holders to run a certain number of cattle over a predetermined area for a specified period of time.

Powers and Smith ranged most of their cattle on the Mojave Desert and in the canyons west of the desert, extending from Indian Wells Canyon to Little Lake Canyon, thirty miles to the north. The Alexander and Robertson herds wintered along Highway 178 from Onyx to Walker

Pass and east of the pass as far as Freeman Junction.

At first glance, putting cattle out to graze on a desert may appear to be a futile endeavor. The dry, dead-looking brush seems incapable of making a good meal for a jackrabbit, much less a cow. Nevertheless, the cattle not only survive, but sometimes actually fatten on their diet of brush, particularly salt brush, which has a great deal of food value. One reason that these herds thrive on the desert in the winter is that they are composed primarily of the "dry" cattle . . . steers, yearlings and cows whose calves have been weaned. When first turned out they still carry some of the fat accumulated during the summer, and their diet of brush is supplemented in the spring by flowering annuals.

When the time came to turn the cattle out on the winter range, Bill and Jim drove their herds together. The drive took about three days. On the way some of the cattle were left scattered near waterholes along the route from Canebrake to Freeman Junction.

Stanley ran some of his cattle in the Canebrake country in winter and spring, and the rest were taken to the desert. On the first day of the drive Stanley took his herd as far as Windmill Field, located a mile and a half below Walker Pass Lodge. On the second day the cattle were driven over Walker Pass to Soldier Wells, a camp on the south side of Highway 178 and about three miles from Highway 14. The south end of Stanley's range was reached on the third day. A few head were dropped off in each of the canyons on the way to Little Lake. This final stage of the drive required one more day.

The route followed by Marvin Powers and his boys was much the same, except that they preferred to take a short-cut. They turned east in back of James place, just below Walker Pass Lodge. Following this canyon, Three Pines Canyon, to the summit, they dropped over into Indian Wells Canyon on the desert side. On the desert, the herd was scattered in the canyons from the Homestead Cafe past Brady's Cafe on Highway 14. The desert canyons which supported Powers and Smith herds ranged from Indian Wells Canyon at the south, northward through Short Canyon, Grapevine, Sand Canyon, No Name, Nine Mile, Dead

Map of Upper South Fork

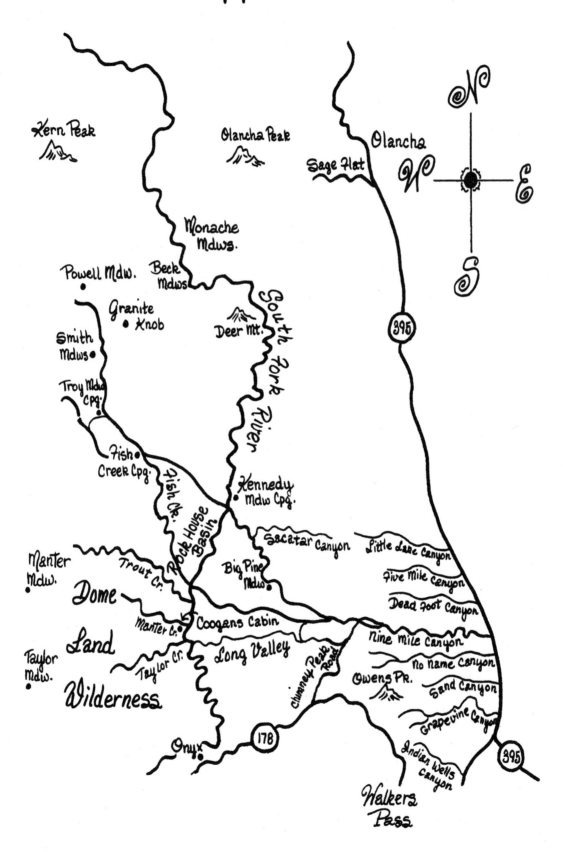

Kern Peak

Olancha Peak

Olancha

Sage Flat

N
W   E
S

Monache Mdws.

Powell Mdw.

Beck Mdws

Granite Knob

Deer Mt.

South Fork River

395

Smith Mdws

Troy Mdw Cpg.

Fish Creek Cpg.

Fish Cr.

Rock House Basin

Kennedy Mdw Cpg.

Sacatar Canyon

Little Lake Canyon

Manter Mdw.

Trout Cr.

Big Pine Mdw

Five Mile Canyon

Dead Foot Canyon

Dome

Nine Mile Canyon

Manter Cr.

Coogans Cabin

No Name Canyon

Land

Taylor Cr.

Long Valley

Chimney Peak Road

Owens Pk.

Sand Canyon

Taylor Mdw.

Wilderness

Grapevine Canyon

Onyx

178

Indian Wells Canyon

395

Walkers Pass

Foot, Five Mile, and finally, Little Lake Canyon.

Before the public domain was reclassified to testing ground by the U. S. Government, the area now occupied by the Naval Weapons Center at China Lake was also grazing land. There were few water holes and this part of the country was generally used only when the wild flowers were at their peak. The flowers contained abundant water in their stalks, enough to sustain the cattle for as long as two weeks without coming in for water.

Powers and Smith had a camp in Grapevine Canyon, just up the canyon past the aqueduct

Stanley Smith rides through Albanita Meadow in the high country.

Sketch by Clint Worlds of an actual happening on the South Fork. Cowboy is Chris Wirth.

70

and on the north side of the creek. Here a cowboy would batch in a small shack, with three or four horses, and possibly a dog, his only company. His life was typical of line camp riders in any cattle country.

Every week or so he checked in at the main ranch to pick up groceries and mail. The rest of the time he was on his own. He rode a different part of the range every day, constantly checking the cattle on each section. When the cows started calving, in March or April, he kept a close eye on any he had reason to believe might have a hard time.

The eyes of a cowboy are his best asset. As he rides, he can watch cattle in the distance and know whether or not everything is as it should be. If the cattle have stopped eating by ten or eleven o'clock in the morning and are lying in the shade of the Joshua trees, indications are that food is plentiful in that area.

An ability to interpret cattle tracks also helps the cowboy to ascertain the condition of his herd. A weak cow, one which perhaps has had trouble calving, leaves a distinctive set of tracks. Most cowboys can tell by looking at tracks how many cattle have moved across a certain area, how long ago, and the size and condition of the cattle.

In the movies, the horse ridden by the cowboy hero is depicted as a kind of equine Boy Scout . . . gentle, faithful, intelligent, helpful, kind, loving . . . a cowboy's best friend. So much for Hollywood. The truth is that many are just the opposite. Many a lone line rider has been seriously injured while riding young unbroken colts or horses with cantankerous dispositions. Some horses, like some people, are born mean. They will wait day after day just to catch a cowboy off guard. They will scheme for a chance to buck him off, kick him, or worse yet, buck him off and head back to camp, leaving the rider to hoof it across the desert. To a cowboy, this is the final humiliation. Most of them have no use whatever for walking, and will mount a horse to go a distance no greater than fifty feet.

There have been instances where a cowboy has been bucked off and lain injured for one or more days before being discovered by someone from the main ranch. Such incidents are accepted philosophically as part of the game, an

Leaving the Smith Ranch in 1915 for the high country; Tommy Smith, *right*, and Hattie Smith, *in the middle.*

occupational hazard. A cowboy would feel uneasy if he thought the bosses were too concerned about his physical well-being. He has other things to worry about, and so do they.

From November through May, before the heat of the summer, the climate of the desert is ideal. Cold, crisp nights are followed by sunny days perfumed with the fragrance of sagebrush and, in the spring, wildflowers. The occasional dust storms or, at times, snow flurries, only serve to keep a man on his toes.

Sometimes more than one man was left at the Grapevine Camp. Such was the case with Clint Worlds, renowned cowboy artist, who camped with one of the Powers boys. One of Clint's favorite evening pastimes was to sketch the day's happenings—a wild bull roped or his partner getting bucked from a bronc — on pieces of cardboard box or anything handy while Powers gave his advice, which was really not needed. Clint also went to the high country for Smith and was a natural artist. His work was made so much better by completely knowing his field. Like most cowboys, he was a little eccentric at times.

He once startled Powers out of a sound sleep by shooting his 1934 Ford full of holes when it failed to start fast enough for an unscheduled trip to town. Another time, while at Fish Creek Camp, he attempted to show the boys how he could spur a bucking horse in the neck while perched on the hitching rack. He succeeded in getting both spurs caught on top of the rail in front of him and fell on his head in the dust.

Many of these incidents followed the sampling of cough medicine. These events did not occur too often, and those who did use the hard stuff occasionally did not let it interfere with their work. For a time Worlds worked in Calico Ghost Town as an artist, but in later years his work took him to New Mexico. Some of his early sketches were saved by Kern Valley residents. Most, though, have disappeared over the years.

In May, the Powers-Smith cattle started moving on their own toward Nine Mile Canyon. The crews came in and started working the range, driving everything ahead of them toward the summer pastures. Complicating the work of the cowboys were those cattle, and there were always a few, which did not care to be driven *anywhere*. They bunched up among the willows along the canyon bottom. In this dense, rattlesnake-infested brush the men were obliged to dismount and work the cows through on foot.

As the Powers-Smith herd approached Chimney Meadow, at the eastern edge of the Kern Plateau, they would begin to intermingle with the Alexander-Robertson cattle being worked up from Canebrake. Camp was set up at Chimney, occupied by about fifteen cowboys and cowgirls. Each shared the daily chores of camp life, from wrangling horses in the early morning to carrying water and cutting piñon pine for cooking. There were no roads into this country until 1930. All supplies and necessities were packed in on mules. Groceries packed into the high country were usually left in the kyacks or pack boxes which served as primitive cupboards.

From Chimney, the combined herd was driven on toward the South Fork of the Kern River. Some of the cows were so eager to reach the high country that they would abandon their calves. Some, of course, had to be driven every step of the way.

The beef — a big part of the meals for the men and women participating in the drive — was furnished by the permittees, the amount contributed being based upon the amount of cattle each man ran. For instance, Stanley Smith ran about 500 head, while Powers, Alexander, and Robertson, combined, had aproximately 700 head. Therefore, as the butchering was done on a prorated basis, Stanley provided almost half of the beef.

Butchering usually took place in the evening. A fat heifer calf weighing about 500 pounds was driven into camp. One man would rope her by the head, holding the calf by taking turns of the rope around the saddle horn. Then a second cowboy would come in and catch one or two hind feet in his loop. With the animal stretched out between the two ropes, another cowboy would tap her between the eyes with the back of a single-bit axe. The throat was cut immediately and the beef was bled quickly and completely.

The animal was then rolled on its back under a piñon tree, supported on either side by blocks to prevent it from rolling, and four men would begin skinning. A cut through the hide was made down the middle of the stomach from the head to the tail; the hide then would be slit from this initial cut up the inside of each leg. Normally one man would work on each leg, skinning it out and cutting the foot off at the first joint while leaving it attached to the hide. With the legs skinned out, they would progress down the sides to the back. The beef was rolled from side to side to facilitate removal of the hide. During removal, care was taken that the ears be left intact to assure there would be no question as to who had contributed the animal. After removal of the entrails, a gamble stick of oak, usually about two feet long, was inserted into holes cut above the hock of each hind leg. The gamble stick was then attached with a chain to a block and tackle and the beef raised to a convenient working level.

Almost none of the beef was wasted. In addition to the liver, heart, and sweetbreads, the marrow guts were considered a delicacy in cow camp. This is part of the intestine of a suckling calf which is filled with marrow-like substance. One calf may produce three or four feet of usable material. A knot is tied at each end to preserve the marrow, and the entire thing, along with the other edible entrails were soaked overnight in salt water. It was then sliced into two-inch sections for cooking, rolled in seasoned flour, and fried crisp.

The beef was trimmed and, with all excess fat removed, was put into a large meat bag. It was then hung overnight and allowed to chill in the crisp mountain air. The next morning it was cut into quarters, returned to the meat sack, and wrapped in bed rolls to protect it from the heat of the day. The process of hanging to chill each night and wrapping during the day was used in place of a refrigerator, and worked every bit as good. With many people in camp, it would be gone within ten days.

After all edibles had been removed from the entrails and the brain taken from the skull cavity, a cowboy would put a rope on the head and unusable entrails, and would drag them into the brush a quarter-mile from camp. There they made a feast for coyotes, who could be heard from camp that night, yelping and howling their appreciation for the meal.

The cabin at Chimney was packed in during a snow storm in 1920.

"Caviatha" or horse herd grazing on Chimney.

Each day of the drive started early with the typical cow camp breakfast of bacon, eggs, biscuits or hot cakes, fried potatoes, pink beans and fresh beef liver, brains, and so forth. With such an early start, the work would generally be finished by three o'clock in the afternoon. There always seemed to be seven or eight children in camp. After the day's ride they amused themselves by practicing their roping, or looking for Indian arrowheads and other artifacts.

The older children could usually coax or bully one of the smaller fry to take the part of the calf in the roping practice. The little one would run while the others would attempt to rope his feet. The ropers never tired of the game, but a halt was called when the make-believe calf ran out of steam, or was jerked down hard once too often.

It is rare that four families could work and live so closely for so many years without major differences arising. Life at camps such as Chimney Meadows and the South Fork of the Kern River prove that it can be done. It may have been a good combination of personalities.

The little cabin at Chimney Meadows measured about ten by twenty feet. Lumber for this cabin was packed in on mules over two feet of snow during March of 1920. Mort S. Hall pre-cut and packaged the cabin at the ranch. It was hauled to the foot of the hill by wagon, then packed on the mules to Chimney. The cabin was of single-wall construction, of 1-inch by 12-inch boards on a 2-inch by 4-inch frame. There was no insulation, and the floor, of one-by-twelves, was covered with black roofing paper. In later years it was ceiled, insulated, and had a new floor installed. But in the old days it turned mighty cold inside when the wind whistled up the canyon and the fog hung low.

At one end of the cabin was a large wood-burning cookstove. Along one side, below two double windows, was an eight foot long table, flanked by benches. A smaller table near the stove, and a double bed in the corner, completed the furnishings. The bed was usually allotted to one of the older couples. Everyone else slept out under the stars.

In the 1940's a small barn in which to store hay was built of corrugated sheet metal below the house. This caused Stanley to say to Marvin, "Did I tell you I built a barn at Chimney?" Marvin, who was always a great kidder, replied, "You had a barn, why didn't you build a house?"

Although rattlesnakes were encountered almost every day on the desert, they were a special hazard at the camps at Chimney and the South Fork. Every time someone came into camp, he had to walk rather cautiously until he had checked it out for snakes. You can bet the beds were checked before climbing in at night, too.

Almost everyone had a bedroll . . . the forerunner of the sleeping bag. Components of the bedroll were a piece of heavy canvas about sixteen feet long and eight feet wide, a mattress two or three inches thick, blankets, quilts, sheet blankets, and a pillow. Some beds had so many quilts a man could barely throw it on top of the pack.

The canvas was spread on the ground, then the mattress was placed on the upper part so that the remainder of the canvas could be folded over toward the center, and the snaps that were affixed to the outside edges were fastened together in the center. For transportation or storage, the centers were snapped, the bedroll rolled tightly, and then neatly tied with a small rope.

Cowboys always took their clothes to bed under the canvas to keep them free of the morning dew. Damp Levis at daybreak are a shock to the system. Those who retired before dark or arose after daylight soon became quite adept at dressing and undressing under the canvas as there were no dressing rooms. It has been said that humans dress up, and cowboys dress down. The hat would go on first; next the shirt, if taken off—which most were not. A Levi jacket would follow, to guard against morning chill. Pants were pulled on, then socks. Boots were the only item of dress to be put on after the canvas was thrown back.

As the last of the herd approached the South Fork, camp was moved from Chimney Meadows to the River. Before the Nine Mile Road was built in 1930, this move entailed transporting all necessary gear fifteen miles on mules. After that time, trucks were used.

The river camp was much less luxurious than that at Chimney. It consisted entirely of a wood stove on a small, sandy beach above the Kern. When the drive to the mountains was on, usually toward the last of June, the weather was mild enough to make camping in the open quite enjoyable. Bringing the cattle out in the fall, with snow flying, was something else again.

Two small cabins have since been built at the river camp, the first of which burned down. They were nothing elaborate, but simply shelter from weather and a place to cook and eat. The South Fork folks have been a hardy breed, and most prefer sleeping in the open rather than under a roof.

The loose horses were driven to the river from Chimney. There were usually more than forty head, all eager to be on the move. It was all that one man could do to hold them to a lope or even a fast trot. It never took long to cover the distance between camps.

Once at the river, the horses were turned into a 100-acre field. A wrangling horse remained in a smaller field close to camp. Each morning, shortly after daylight, one of the children would ride out and run the horses back into a corral near the camp. The kids took turns at this detail. Many a wild ride was taken over the sagebrush as the young rider ran the wrangling horse full tilt in an effort to turn the willful horses who had decided against confinement.

During the four or five days camp was set up at the river, cattle continued to be brought up from the winter range. The South Fork of the Kern River forms the boundary between lands under the jurisdiction of the Bureau of Land Management and those of the Forest Service.

The cattle are worked to arrive at the river on a date set by the Forest Service, at which time they may be counted onto the high country summer range. Counting through the drift fence usually begins around July 1st. A drift fence was designed, as the name implies, to prevent cattle from drifting onto a range where they did not belong or off a range where they do.

In the 1940s, a man by the name of Calahan took over the old Chet Smith homestead down Big Pine Creek. This site later became known as The Old Baldy Scout Ranch. Calahan had a primitive sort of a night club there and, as it was only a twenty-minute drive from the river camp, some of the young cowboys occasionally would jump in a pick-up to go take a look at the bright lights. It was a popular spot for many from the big city.

One who spent quite a bit of time at Calahans was Stuart Hamblin. He had a pack of hounds and used to hunt bear and lion while staying there. On one of his hunting trips to this area he stumbled onto the homesteader's cabin, which prompted him to write the song "This Old House."

Cattle were counted at two locations, both of which were established around 1910. One was southwest of the river bridge, and the other above Kennedy Meadow Campground. While the physical sites have remained the same, the coming of roads has had a pronounced effect on the original character of this land.

The cattle were bunched near the gate through which they were to pass. As the animals crowded through a few at a time, a cattleman—usually Stanley—stood on the left of the gate, calling out the brand of each animal. A Forest Ranger noted each brand on a tally sheet, as it was called. Each cattleman was allowed to graze a certain number of head as specified in his permit. For this number, the Forest Service charged so many cents per head per month. Only the grown cattle were counted. Calves under six months of age were given a free ride on National Forest pasturage.

The animals counted through at Kennedy Campground headed up river into the country south of Monache Meadows. Those which passed through the southern gate worked their way up toward Rodeo Flat and into the area north of Fish Creek and Troy Meadow Campground.

The range used by the four Fish Creek permittees encompassed thirty square miles—or 90,000 acres—with much being too mountainous and rocky for cattle. These cattlemen and their families know most of these acres intimately. The areas that they did not enter during their summer cattle work, they covered while deer hunting or fishing—and the people loved each mountain meadow and timbered slope. The four permittees, being God-fearing men, and with the realization that they were only leasing this portion of the Forest, felt as though they were entrusted with the safe-keeping of this vast acreage by God.

The boundaries of the summer range were Monache Meadows and the Monache drift fence on the north; Beach Ridge on the west, where the ridge acted as a natural barrier; and, Bald Mountain to the south, again unfenced—the border being Bald Mountain Saddle. Usually only about 1,200 head of grown stock were run on the combined permits.

Four summer camps were used by the cattlemen and their families. Bill Alexander's was at Powell Meadow; Marvin Powers' at Granite Knob; and the Smith and Robertson's on upper Fish Creek—all about a mile apart.

Everyone concerned looked forward throughout the winter and spring to the day when it would be time for the outfits to move into the high country. As many as twenty adults and children would make up the party. Age was no barrier; babies rode on pillows in front of their parents, or were comfortably settled in well-padded kyaks firmly secured to a mule. At least ten pack mules or horses completed the entourage. Pack animals carrying quantities of bedding and other light, bulky objects seemed to all but disappear under the load, looking more like a huge bedroll with legs, ears, and tail.

Though cattlemen were expert packers, packing time was always hectic, at best. Having been idle for five or six months, there was ample time for some mules to work up a distinct aversion to carrying anything other than their own natural hides.

Snow and freezing weather wreaked havoc with fences. The first job on arrival in the high country was to repair the fence on the wrangling pasture. This was a small pasture, usually about half an acre, in which a horse could be caught quickly and used to run in the other horses. After the wrangling pasture was secured, the other fences were tended to.

The summer camps were at an elevation of approximately 8,000 feet. The nights were cold and the days were glorious. When the cattle first came into the mountains in the spring, the snow was almost entirely melted, with just a patch or two remaining in heavily timbered areas. The growing season was short at this elevation but it seemed that Mother Nature made allowances for this by accelerating the cycle to the point where one could almost see the grass and flowers grow. A hundred varieties of flowers bloomed in the mountain meadows, their fragrance mingling with the spicy scent of the pines.

The fishing done by the younger generation at the South Fork camp was insignificant when compared with the thrill of catching the wary golden trout of the high country. The streams were small and in some spots almost overgrown. Most originated from springs some distance on up the mountain. The fish were small, being normally only six to eight inches—just frying-pan size. They were usually hungry, too. One fish per cast was almost a guarantee.

All the horses were kept at Stanley Smith's field until the other men could repair their fences, then they were moved to the individual pastures. The men lucky enough to go early with the horses would quickly patch up the fence around the horse pasture or wrangling field, then grab a fishing pole and head for the creek. It was considered an honor to bring in the first limit of trout for the year. Soon the rest of the outfit arrived, and moved on to their individual camps. By sundown there would be fish in each camp. The aroma of trout fried in bacon grease would drift from each cooking fire the next morning.

The ranchers pooled their manpower in order to get their fences repaired as quickly as possible. This usually took four or five days, giving the cattle time to reach the meadows and rest up for the spring branding. Branding time was the highlight of the year for most of those involved, and particularly for the younger folks. Many of the kids would rather rope than eat, and never seemed to get enough of it during the rest of the year. Branding corrals were set up at various locations on the range, so that the scattered cattle would not have to be driven any great distance.

Seven o'clock in the morning found all hands assembled at Stanley Smith's camp. Stanley, the rodeo boss, would then inform them of the plans for the day. If the branding was to take place at Beck Meadows, for instance, Stanley might have said something like this:

"Bill and Leonard, go through Corral Meadows and work the country around Little Bull Meadows. Come out at the head of Beck and meet us at the rodeo ground. Marvin, you take your boys and work Lost Meadow —pushing them down Lost Creek to Beck. Jim, you and your family work the country around Swallow Point and along the drift fence. I'll take my outfit and ride through the Inyo County cattle on the other side of Monache drift fence. We'll pick up any of the cattle that might have gotten through the fence."

Usually the instructions were not even as lengthy as this. Everyone knew what was expected when riding a certain part of the country. Any of the others could have made these decisions, but Stanley had been chosen and he did a good job.

The work generally followed the same pattern, year after year. Seven days were needed to complete the branding, one day being spent at each of the following meadows: Albanita, Broder, Beck, Smith, Jackass, and Troy. Each location had its branding corral, built of logs. The seventh day was pick-up day, when men would scatter over the range and drive any unbranded calves and their mothers back to Fish Creek. They would be branded at Smith Meadow and turned loose.

Each rider or group of riders would complete his circle by ten or eleven o'clock and begin arriving at the rodeo ground. When all riders were accounted for, one of the permittees would begin to cut out his cows and calves. The cattle were maintained in a loose bunch, as the cattlemen cut out their cows and unmarked calves. Each moved his stock in a different direction away from the main herd, and kept them separate to await their turn in the branding corral. Cutting from the herd was over by noon, and the branding fire was started.

A mule loaded with brands, medicine, and lunch was usually led out to the branding site. This was one of the few times when the cattlemen ate lunch when out riding. A coffee pot on the branding fire would produce the brew to accompany anything from bean sandwiches to cold trout or steak, cold biscuits, canned tomatoes or peaches, and big squares of Hershey's chocolate.

Now branding began. The smallest group of calves was taken to the branding corral first in order to free the men holding them. As soon as their cut or bunch was branded and turned loose, they helped with the others.

There was something intriguing about calf branding that was hard to explain. In a setting of pine-fringed meadows and crystal clear streams, the age-old ritual was even more fascinating. Picture, if you will, the milling, bawling cattle held a short distance away, a log corral full of calves, cowboys and cowgirls doing the jobs they came to do. Smoke from the branding fire ascending high in the unbelievably clear sky. A calf was marked with its owner's brand, a puff of pungent smoke, and the calf ran bawling to its mother. Each phase of the operation combined to create a scene that was eagerly anticipated by even old-timers who had taken part in the annual event all their lives.

Two to four men worked in the corral on horseback, roping the calves. When two men worked together, the one who caught the last calf by the hind feet would give his partner the

Branding at Fish Creek in 1941. Bill Alexander on horseback.

first throw at the next calf. If he missed his first throw, either man was free to try. Some of the top ropers have roped for hours at a time and never missed catching both hind feet with every loop that left their hand. However, it was observed that no matter how fast a man could get another loop built, or how good a roper his partner was, he would give the other man first shot at the hind feet if he had caught the last one. This was part of the unwritten code of the West.

As one man caught the calf by the hind feet and dragged it to the fire, the second man roped the animal by the head. If the calf was very small, the second rope was not used until reaching the fire—at which time the calf would be flanked or thrown. A rope was put on its front feet, and the animal stretched out. That is, each horse maintained enough tension on the rope to prevent the calf from kicking loose.

In working cattle, the horse was all-important. Whether in or out of the corral, a good roping horse put a rider in the best position to make his throw and kept the rope taut at all times after the catch had been made. A good cow horse did many small but important details on his own. It was a joy to ride such a good horse or to watch him perform. A good roper became infinitely better on a horse with enough savvy to give his rider every advantage.

The branding fire was located inside the gate of the larger corrals and outside the smaller ones. When a calf reached the fire, a crew of

Branding calves at Troy Meadow in 1970. Jimmy Andreas brands while Sundy Andreas looks on.

77

four or five men, women, and kids went to work. Most difficult of the chores was to flank the calf or tail it down. A great deal of teamwork was required to get a big, ten-month old calf to the ground. If the heeler caught both hind feet, the header would put his loop on the head, and the calf would be pulled to the ground by the tail. But if only one foot was caught, a rope was many times put on the head too. One man would grab the rope to the hind foot on the opposite side to which he was standing, another cowboy would then grab the calf's tail and as they gave a pull together the animal's free leg was jerked out from under it.

The ropers would let a little slack in the rope. The calf was jerked down. The man who had the tail jumped to the shoulder of the calf and pulled its front foot back and upward, bracing his knees against the calf's neck and shoulders. The other flanker pulled the calf's tail between its legs and, maintaining a steady pull, reached forward with one hand to remove the rope from the hind foot. Crossing the hind feet, he put the loop back on and then held it tight until the roper had taken his turns on the horn with his rope—or "dallied," as it is called—and backed his horse. The man who held the front foot took the rope off the head, crossed the front feet, slipped the loop around them, and the calf was ready to work on.

Registered brands are generally placed on the left side of the animal, so the calf is stretched out on its right side. Each family usually handled the branding and earmarking of its own calves. By the time a child was twelve or thirteen years old, he could do all of the tasks involved in branding—and do them well.

First shot at the grounded calf went to the man who did the ear-marking and castrating. It takes about one minute to castrate a bull calf. The by-products of the procedure, called "mountain oysters," were collected by one of the kids. They were then cooked on the coals at the edge of the branding fire, and eaten on the spot. A roper who had a spare minute would ride over to get his share. They were consumed, as is, unsalted and unseasoned. The taste is similar to frog legs or chicken.

The earmark is a great deal more important than the brand, as it can be seen and recog-

nized at a distance of up to a quarter of a mile. In the winter, when the hair on the hide is fairly long, a brand is relatively difficult to read. But a well-made earmark is easily discernible.

Each cattleman has his earmark made in a particular way, and those who perform the operation make certain to mark it just that way. Marvin Powers used an earmark like this. His brand was a circle dot on the left hip. Stanley Smith used and the 13 brand on the left hip. Jim Robertson used with the bar wrench brand on the left hip. This brand was patterned after the old wagon wrench used to remove the wheel nuts. Bill Alexander's earmark was a . His brand called the Seven H.L., was placed on the left ribs.

While the marker worked on the head, the calf was vaccinated against Black Leg Fever and branded. Each brand was usually placed correctly, but occasionally one of the kids would slip and the brand was positioned too high or too low. Whoever misplaced the brand would be reminded of it every time that particular animal showed up on the range. As the brand was put on with a rocking motion the smoke turned from brown to blue. This indicated that the hair was burned through, hide had been reached, and a good brand achieved.

Stanley Smith always dehorned his calves as he earmarked. He felt that they were easier to feed in winter and would bring a little more at market without horns. The others claimed that the cows could more readily keep the coyotes away from small calves if allowed to keep

Bob Powers roping calves on Cedar.

their horns. Pine tar was applied to the open cut on the bull calves, and to the head if the calf had been dehorned. This was done to keep flies away. In years when the screw worms were bad, even the earmark was dabbed and the calves had to be watched closely all summer. Many times they had to be roped and doctored out on the range if they showed signs of having worms. A calf seen shaking his head or wringing his tail was most likely needing attention. This is where experience was most valuable, as a cowhand could usually tell the condition of cattle simply by observing them as he rode past.

Branding proceeded at a fast clip and, although nobody seemed to be rushing, there was no lost motion as, on most branding days, there was a long ride back to camp afterwards. At Beck Meadows, this involved about a ten-mile ride. The youngsters used to slip off in the lead and race down through the timbered slopes, jumping logs and dodging limbs. This was not a very safe sport, and not the best thing in the world for the horses, some of which were spoiled in this way. They became so inclined that they would always want to run to camp. No one was ever seriously injured, though. A little hide taken off was considered to be part of the game.

A good horse under a cowboy makes a good cowhand even better. Every cattleman had his favorite horses that he owned during his lifetime. Bill Aleck's favorites were Buck, Johnny, and Sleepy. Jim swore by Butch and Baldy. With Marvin it was Frenchy, Cowboy, and Cedar. Stanley's many favorites included Pe-

dro, Frank, Joker, Sheik, Smokey, Napoleon, and Chico. These horses never won prizes at the County Fair, but many of them could have. They were top working horses, which could carry a man all day.

Sometimes on the fall trips one horse would be ridden every day for a week. This really showed how much stamina a horse had. Those horses that did win ribbons were good at one thing. The working cow horses, however, never specialized, but most were equally skilled at roping, cutting, and carrying the cowboy at any speed through rough country as he made his daily ride. The South Fork cattlemen were blessed with many fine riders who worked with them over the years. It would be impossible to name all of them, but a few outstanding men come to mind.

Brock Cole worked for all of the cattlemen at one time or another. Brock had a lot of tall tales to tell. He had the gift of gab and kept up a constant chatter. He was well liked by all as there was never a dull moment when he was around. Tough as a hickory nut, Brock would make the fall trip into the mountains wearing a light shirt and old jumper. Most of the others would have long underwear, chaps and heavy coats, yet still seem to feel the cold more than Brock. Brock was always getting off his horse and setting a sagebrush afire—which was the only thing that indicated he might be cold.

Freddy Burke and Alphonso Ridarte rode for Jim Robertson for many years, as did William Peterson for Bill Alexander. Another old-timer, an Arizona cowboy named Harvey Robinson, rode herd on the Alexander-Robertson cattle while on the winter and summer range. Jimmy and Johnny Chico often helped Marvin Powers with the cattle, as did Art Cole and Hoot McDonald. Stanley Smith had the biggest bunch of cattle, and so he hired more outside help, many of whom worked year around for Smith. These men were not only top hands when it came to working the cattle and horses, but also were welcome additions in the cow camps, where they helped on everything from washing dishes to cutting wood. Among those who will be longest remembered were Paul Rhoads, Smiley Ramos, Red Vega, Willie Andreas, Tony Pablo, and Walt Mecham. Others who worked for shorter periods for Smith were Buster

Red Vega *on the left;* Smiley Ramos *on the right;* when they were riding for the Smith Ranch.

Paul Rhoads washing his clothes at Smith's Meadow on Fish Creek.

More money was put into boots than any other item of clothing. Most of the riders ordered through Western or Bloocher Boot Companies, where their measurements were kept on record. Some of the men wore a small silk scarf around their neck. When water had to be carried from the creek, heated on a wood stove, and clothes hand scrubbed, shirts were not changed every time a bit of mud got on them. The Levi pants seldom got as much washing as other articles of clothing. Some of the younger cowboys actually preferred to wear them without washing until they were almost completely worn out. They could step out of them, and the pants would stand by themselves. As long as they didn't try to walk off by themselves they were not considered too dirty. Although seldom washed, they were *dry cleaned* almost daily. This consisted of scraping off everything, including corral dirt, with one's pocket knife. More than one young bride found herself in hot water by deciding her cowboy husband needed to have all his Levis washed.

The time spent in camp was also used to care for any horses needing shoeing, although this was done many times when the men came back to camp early from a regular day's ride. The horses had to be reshod every six weeks or so, and each rancher took care of his own horses. Most had learned to shoe horses as boys watch-

Rhoads, Ray Milligan, Sid Andreas, and Lyman Peterson.

After the branding had been finished at all locations, everyone would take a few days off in camp. This gave time to check over clothing that needed washing. Most of the cattle people dressed about the same. Levis were usually worn, along with blue cotton workshirts. Long handled underwear was substituted for the conventional type, much of the time for extra warmth. Unlined Levi jackets were popular and, when not being worn, were tied behind the saddle. The cowman's hat had as much personality as the man himself, and were discarded only when completely worn out. Everyone who rode on the Fish Creek range remembers how Bill Aleck put his hat on and then pulled it down and around as if he were screwing it on, so that the front always faced a little to the side.

80

Don Powers on Topsey at Fish Creek.

ing their dads. Often there would be some genuine excitement around camp when a colt or one of the broke horses was being shod that did not quite like the idea. None were too tough to handle, and, although gentleness was the rule, it was considered okay to attract their attention by whacking them along the ribs with a shoeing rasp. A hind foot might have to be tied up or an animal thrown to the ground to get shoes on him, but this was the exception. If the horse was started right, he usually accepted the shoeing process as part of the routine.

A few days off were also used to wash saddle blankets and make repairs on their riding gear. Great care was taken with the horse's back. Saddles were not only bought to fit well, but clean saddle blankets were a must. Many cattlemen used a two-fold Navajo blanket next to the saddle and a three-fold wool blanket next to the horse's back — turned and re-folded as it got dirty. Two sets of blankets were generally on hand so that one could be washed while the other was in use. Prior to being saddled, the animals always received a good brushing on the back and other parts covered by the saddle. On a long, hot pull, the men would get off and, after loosening the cinch, prop the back of their saddle up by resting an elbow on the horse's back. This allowed a little air onto the mount's back.

Although many types of bits were used, many of the riders favored the Spanish or spade bit. Most popular were those made by Abie Hunt, a pioneer Kern County bit maker. These bits may look inhumane, but if made and used right a horse gets used to the feel of one in his mouth and can be kept with a "light mouth" all his life.

Split leather reins were used to a good degree, but some leaned toward the use of braided rawhide or leather reins, with romel attached. Rawhide reatas were carried by most of the old-timers in lieu of the newer grass or nylon ropes. But as it became harder to get good rawhide work done, they gradually switched over. Jim Robertson, the last old-timer to pack a rawhide reata on the Fish Creek range, used this type of rope until his retirement. Willie Nicoll was remembered as being an artist with a reata. Carrying a 50-footer, he would

Jim Robertson in front of his cabin at Fish Creek in 1919.

swing an eight-foot loop and reach out for an unbelievably long distance, seldom missing.

Some of the hands occasionally broke down and took a bath. One such event that took place at Smith's camp will be long remembered. The men were butchering beef. After letting the men know in which direction they were headed, a couple of young school teachers and some of the other young ladies headed up the creek. A quarter mile up, and well out of sight, was a good sandy pool, about knee deep and five or six feet across. On one side was a big flat rock on which to dry off.

This was in the 1930's and the pool was twenty miles from the nearest road, so there was not a chance in a thousand that anyone would ride up on them. There simply was nobody except cattlemen in that part of the country. No bathing suits were packed into the mountains, yet they felt as safe as if at the Y.W.C.A. They had taken their baths and were sunning themselves on the rock. Back at camp someone got a bright idea; one of the women in the camp would ride up the creek and give the girls a scare. Gwen Smith, always a good sport, volunteered to do the honors. The girls knew that the entrails of the butchered animal would be dragged out that way, but figured the men would wait until they were back in camp.

Riding Red Vega's horse, Buddy, and wearing Red's hat and jumper, Gwen broke through the small trees near the swimming hole, head down, and dragging the entrails. The ladies were laughing and talking and thereby did not

Smith's Cabin at Fish Creek. In front of the cabin are, *from the left,* Tommy Smith, Preston Powers, Ramon Bencoma, Jack Powers and Sam Cuddeback. Three men on far left are unidentified.

see Gwen until she was fifty or sixty feet away. When spotted, from what Mrs. Smith says, it was really a sight to see those girls all try to hide in that little, shallow pool.

A lot of good-natured kidding went on around the camps. This included anything from finding your bed in the top of a pine tree to having a coiled rope placed under your bed and pulled out slowly just as you were going to sleep. Although rattlesnakes were not too bad at this elevation, they were quite thick in the lower country. The sensation of having a snake in bed with you caused many a rapid change of location. Generally these people were a happy bunch, doing what they enjoyed, and working as a family group.

With branding finished, and everyone rested up, the group headed back to the Valley to put up the second cutting of hay. One man stayed behind to watch the cattle. Almost everyone hated to leave, but there was very little time in this cattle operation to spend loafing in the high country. The worst part was having to ride back down into the heat of the South Fork after three or four weeks of ideal daytime temperature.

After about three weeks in the Valley, the work in the hayfields was finished. The families headed back to the high country. Most of them took guests along. Many of these guests cherished the memories of beef gathering at Fish Creek.

Each of the cattlemen, with the exception of Stanley Smith, used a gathering field furnished by the Forest Service. Stanley owned his own meadow at Fish Creek. By coming up Fish Creek, the first camp along the way was Jim Robertson's. Jim built a comfortable cabin, about 10 by 18 feet, and a cook shed in front, for Ann and himself. Except in the fall, not too much time was spent in the cabin when the hands were there. Usually everyone sat around the cooking area. There was a good wood cookstove both under the cook shed and inside the cabin. Most of the kitchen utensils were hung on nails from the cabin wall or on the wall at the back of the shed.

These mountaineers could put out a good meal with a cast-iron frying pan, one kettle, a Dutch oven, and a coffee pot. And they put it out in a hurry. Anyone who has ever camped at Robertson's remembers Jim's Dutch oven biscuits. Dutch oven cooking is an art that has all but disappeared, and Jim was a master at it. The Dutch oven is a cast iron kettle, 10 inches to 24 inches across. A rim around the lid held the coals. Some had short legs, though these were not necessary. There were two types of cooking done in a Dutch oven. By burying the oven in a pit and leaving it for four or five hours you could cook a batch of beans, roast, or stew, or anything that required a long time. By the other method, you baked in the open. Such things as biscuits and pies baked in this fashion were hard to beat.

For biscuits, a fire was built ahead of time. As the fire burned down to coals, the oven and lid were preheated. The inside of the oven was treated in a very special way. Old-time cooks never washed the inside, in order to preserve the interior conditioning or seasoning, as it was called. If it ever became necessary to wash the oven, the interior was reconditioned by heating the oven and rubbing a raw potato into the pores of the metal. A wooden hook was used to place the oven where you wanted it. The oven was carried by hooking the metal bail, and the lid was carried by the small handle on top.

Stanley Smith's cabin was small, about 8 by 16 feet. It was built by an old-timer named Ed Pettypool, in 1900. In 1928, the year Stanley and Gwen were married, a sign was hung over the door: "You have had your wedding bells. From now on it's cow bells and tin cans." It hung over the door for forty years, and finally the weather finished it.

Sitting at the 12-foot tables in the cook shed, you could look down across a 100-acre meadow. In the evening, sometimes as many as twenty deer would cautiously enter the meadow. Groundhogs napped in the sun around Ground Hog Point, a pile of rocks that stuck out into the meadow, or early in the morning you could watch one of the kids running the horses across the frosty meadow as they worked their way through the sagebrush and into the pines to the corral.

This was always done at a dead run. If the horses were brought in slow, they would try to break back. The wrangle horse was usually ridden bare-back. The kids could ride like little Indians, their horses dodging trees and jumping logs, sagebrush and creeks.

A large range or cookstove stood at the north end of the cook shed. It was quite a job to get it up to the camp. Even after it was stripped of all removable parts, it weighed 400 pounds, and had to be packed in on a mule the last eighteen miles.

A big gray mule named Dick did the honors. Although he tried to buck it off before it was tied down, he went all the way with the stove. This was the heaviest load ever packed into the back country by an animal. Dick's fame did not last long, however. The following year he was bitten in the face by a rattlesnake as he reached for a mouthful of grass, and died from the bite. The big range had a grill on each side. Tons of beef steaks cooked on them were without equal, even in restaurants where the cost of a good steak was exhorbitant.

There was always a big, black, two-gallon coffee pot at the back of the stove. As the fire almost never went out during the waking hours, you could get a cup of hot coffee anytime. A little more water and a little more coffee were added until the grounds built up too far. At that point they were thrown out, the pot rinsed, and coffee making started again. This coffee had real body to it and could not be duplicated by any of the modern methods.

Wood for cooking was never a problem. Some of the crew would go out on the hill above camp and fell a dead lodge-pole pine—occasionally referred to as "tamarack"—about thirty inches through, with a two-man hand-saw called a "misery whip."

Smith's Meadow at Fish Creek in 1941, as seen from the cabin. Cattle are being worked on sand bar to the left. Rocky point on far right is Groundhog Point. Large rocky knob on skyline is Granite Knob.

The limbs that did not break when it fell were chopped off and hauled into camp on a home-made sled called a stone boat, pulled by one of the pack mules. These limbs, called "squaw wood," were two to five inches in diameter, and made an excellent cooking fire. It could be broken easily into desired lengths by popping it over a log. Keeping the wood box filled was a chore that usually belonged to the youngsters. They also were in charge of carrying water from the spring, wrangling the horses, and milking the cow if there happened to be one in camp.

At the Powers' camp, cooking was done in the open until the 1930's. Then Marvin and his boys put up a small, sheet-metal cabin. The main attraction of this cabin was a Home Comfort cook stove. The biscuits and golden trout for breakfast or haunch of venison cooked in the oven, to accompany the ever-present pot of beans simmering at the back of the stove, could never be forgotten by those who camped there.

Within 100 yards of the Powers' camp were many trees that had been blown down by heavy winter winds. It was never necessary to cut down a tree or to walk very far for firewood at this camp. A spring bubbled up from white sands fifty yards from camp. A trough was so designed and built that a bucket placed under

Bob Powers stands in the doorway of the small cabin at Granite Knob Meadow.

the trough was soon filled with the coldest, clearest water ever tasted. It was so cold that you had to sip it to avoid setting your teeth on edge.

The Powers' cabin was located at the east edge of Granite Knob Meadow, so as to catch the first rays of the sun filtering through the pines on the chilly summer mornings. The rising sun chased the frost from the meadow, exposing a profusion of wild flowers among the lush grasses.

Tents were provided for those who did not care to sleep in the open. There was never much chance for anyone to oversleep. Just about the time that the sun peeked around Jackass Peak, the squirrels and chipmunks began a self-appointed job of waking everyone in camp. They dropped small pine cones on the tents and ran full-tilt up and down the tent's ridgepole, chattering all the while. They were forgiven at meal times, though, when they would scurry across the dirt floor of the cabin and perch themselves close by to beg for tidbits from the table.

As the first star appeared in the evening, a campfire was built. Not many people stayed up later than nine o'clock because of early rising the next day. Nevertheless, these evenings spent around the fire—with possibly some accordion music by Bill Powers, or a few tunes on the harmonica by Marvin, Sr.—were more pleasant by far than any spent in overstuffed chairs in front of a television set. A poem by Jud Jordan, who spent many a night in this high country, ably conveys the feelings one can hold about this experience.

FISH CREEK CAMP

I've lain in my blankets at nightime
  With the star studded heavens o'er head;
With my camp trappings scattered about me
  And the dying campfire glowing red.
And it seemed that the God who created
  These wonders so long, long ago,
Came close to me there in the silence
  And spoke to me things I should know.
The sage scented breezes of evening
  Came whispering up from the plain,
And the dew, falling soft on the meadow,
  Brought with it the freshness of rain.
The moon riding high in the heavens,
  Bathed the peaks in a mantle of light,
While the tree studded canyons below them
  Lay dark in the stillness of night.
The creek flowing down through the meadow
  Sang a song to night's arches of blue,
And it shone like a ribbon of silver
  Where the pines let the moonbeams drift
    through.
The quavering cry of a coyote
  Came faint on the murmuring breeze,
And my eyelids grew heavy with slumber
  To the whispered good-night of the trees.

             —J. H. JORDAN,
             Bakersfield, California.

Bill Alexander's camp and holding field was located at Powell Meadow, about a mile north of Smith's. Bill and his family required even less in the way of modern conveniences. The only permanent fixtures in their camp were a large homemade stove and table. Built up with rock and cement, the stove had a large cast-iron top with three lengths of stove pipe attached to it. It would take logs up to eight inches in diameter and thirty inches long, and would keep a pot of beans or stew cooking most of the day by filling it in the morning. The lodgepole pine table was about ten feet long, with benches attached, and covered with linoleum. Everything else used in the camp was either stored at Stanley's or packed out each winter.

Try to picture, if you will, sitting down at camp to a good steak or mess of golden trout with Dutch oven biscuits and all the trimmings, while all about was the cool shade of the pines and firs and clean, crisp air. For entertainment there might be a couple of fawns romping on the far side of the meadow, or a coyote out to catch a meal of grasshoppers or gophers, as well as chipmunks scurrying through camp. The saucy bluejays and camp robbers were always around at meal times, their cries and the distant drumming of woodpeckers blending with the murmuring of the mountain stream. Such a setting made good food even better. Many times bears would come into camp at night. They managed to carry off quite a bit of food, and at one time got away with a whole hind quarter of beef.

None of these camps were fancy. But to the families who each summer migrated to the High Sierra with their cattle, it was a second home.

The agreement these cattlemen had with the Forest Service required them to bring part of their herds out of the mountains toward the

Powers family at Fish Creek about 1931. *Left to right*, Bob on Peanut, Isabel holding Bill and riding Jim Pinto, Marvin Sr. on Cowboy, and Marvin Jr. riding Black Bird.

Bill Alexander cooks a meal on the homemade stove at Powell Meadow.

last of August. The exact date varied, being governed by how well the feed was holding up.

The first gathering was handled similar to branding. Each day cattle from a certain part of the range were worked to a central location. Here each permittee cut out forty percent of his cattle to take to the home ranch. Beef cattle were generally selected as, by this time, they were in prime condition. These were taken to the holding pastures at each camp, where they put on a few extra pounds. The meadows were still high with feed, having supported only a few head of saddle horses during the summer.

After the range was completely worked, they began what they called the beef cattle drive. Each family drove its own stock, and usually followed a day behind another drive. The fifty miles to the Valley were covered in about four days, with the families camping along the way.

Care was taken to handle the cattle in a manner which would keep the pounds on them, with very little of the running and jostling depicted in movies. The mark of a good cowboy was his ability to ride hard and fast when the need arose. But to be content to poke along with the cattle while traveling, letting them more or less pick their own speed and keeping them from losing any more weight than was absolutely necessary, this also was quite important as those pounds meant dollars.

Usually Art Alexander at the Onyx Ranch, or his partner, Oscar Rudnick, of Bakersfield, bought the cattle. In the early days cattlemen would deliver the beef cattle to the slaughter

85

house in Bakersfield, which involved an extra 75-mile drive by way of Caliente.

While the cattlemen were in the Valley after this trip, the third cutting of hay was usually put up, provided the river persisted long enough to furnish water for this last crop.

If any part of the year was to be a vacation, it was after the return to the mountains for the last trip. This was usually early in the first part of deer season. The cattlemen had learned years ago that you could not get much work out of a South Fork cowboy until he had a chance to get some of the buck hunting out of his system. Just about everyone hunted, and cattlemen like Marvin and Stanley were the first to understand that, if either of them had a hobby, it was deer hunting. They came by it honestly, since their fathers before them had looked forward to this time of year. So the men usually were given about three days to hunt, with pay. Within a day or two, quite a few bucks were hanging in the shade around the camps. Deer heart and liver would be sizzling in the breakfast pan each morning.

At this time, the youngsters were usually in school, and the wives stayed on the ranch. During this last trip the weather was getting pretty cold, and crawling out into the frosty morning appealed more to the men than to the women, although the latter could endure it if the occasion arose. Not enough can be said about these ranchers' wives—Gwen Smith, Dorothy Alexander, Isabell Powers, and Ann Robertson. All of them rode with the men most of the year and still had time to raise families and do most of the cooking — to say nothing of washing clothes with scrub board and old-time clothes squasher in a washtub heated on a wood fire. Even keeping the children halfway clean in the mountains and where, when they were not riding, the young ones would be sliding down the banks along the creeks or sloshing through the muddy areas of the meadow, was difficult.

The men, therefore, batched on this last trip into the high mountains. As most of them were good camp cooks, they did not suffer too much for want of good food. Cattle were being pushed out of the mountains each day, and as on the trip into the mountains, a lot of the stock would continue on their own once they were stirred and started down the trails. Some cows doubtless would get to thinking about the hay stacks on the ranch and go off and leave their calves.

Being near the end of September and October, the men would camp together at Smith's or Robertson's. Staying up late playing cards or talking—with conversation centering around deer hunting—was the most common form of entertainment. Some of the buck stories dated back to the days when Marvin and Stanley were boys hunting in this same country. One such account related how they went out with only a couple of shells each, for their 32-special rifles. Getting a long shot at a large buck, they wounded him, but spent their shells without killing him. Not wanting to leave him badly wounded, and being too late to go to camp for more ammunition, they tracked him down. As the buck lay half dead from loss of blood, the boys crept up on him. The plan was to grab his head and cut his throat before he could do any damage. As it turned out, he had more life in him than they figured. Two hundred pounds of fury was unleashed in the brush patch, and it looked bad as the boys hung on for dear life wanting so much to turn loose. Their faithful old dog, though, came to the rescue and grabbed the buck by the nose, giving them the chance to cut the buck's throat.

One thing that made buck hunting accounts interesting was the fact that most South Forkers hunted deer Indian style. This meant that once they got on a large buck's track, they stuck with it until they had an opportunity to get in a fatal shot. Their forefathers had hunted the same way, having favorite bucks with names such as Geronimo, Pisano, and Club Foot. These bucks were located each year by their tracks, and hunted until they were killed. Each track was different to these old-timers, and each told a story. The bucks' ultimate fates were sealed after they were tracked and put on the list of those worthy of hunting.

A world of hunting knowledge was acquired by these men in a lifetime. Much of it was picked up from the Indians they grew up with, and who were close friends. The rest was acquired by hundreds of hours spent on the tracks of game until they understood how the buck's mind worked, and I think the deer enjoyed it as much as the hunter. Oftentimes the hunters would kick them out of their beds, and so give them a running chance. And many, such as that master buck hunter, Tommy Smith, never shot them any place but in the neck. Each fall many friends and relatives would go in for these deer hunts, and the warm bond of friendship that was formed during these yearly hunts is portrayed in the following poem written by Jud Jordan, a close friend of Tommy Smith, when Tommy died in 1921:

IN MEMORY OF MY DEAR FRIEND, THE LATE THOMAS S. SMITH

The dear old boy has laid aside
   His saddle, horse and gun
The trails that knew his presence once
   Are riderless by one.

He drifted out one evening
   With an angel by his side
Across the unknown spaces
   Beyond the great divide.

He stole away so softly
   While the stars their vigil kept,
That those who watched beside him
   Scarcely knew but that he slept.

I love you Tommy, dear old boy
   In memory I can see
You riding out across the hills
   And beckoning to me.

I see you leading out along
   The trails we used to know,
That wound far up among the peaks
   And then far down below.

We'll miss you, Companyero,
   On the trails we used to know
We'll miss your smiles and stories
   By the campfire's mellow glow.

And when the campfire flickers low
   And all the long night through
The stars look down upon your camp
   Oh God, how we'll miss you.

Then when the camp's all quiet
   And the punchers are at rest,
We'll breathe a prayer for one who rides
   Far out beyond the west.

And in our dreams we'll be with you
   Upon an antlered track
And follow it along the hill
   Up through the tamarack.

Three old time buck hunters, *left to right*, Jim Powers on Stargo, Ramon Bencoma on Jess, and Tommy Smith on Old Mose, the horse Johnny Powers was riding when Indians killed him in 1891.

The same old packs will lie around
   The camps we used to know
The same old caviatha
   On the meadow down below.

The same camp fire'll be burning
   In the old accustomed place
With the same boys gathered round it,
   But there'll be a vacant place.

The same South Fork's still flowing
   Through the Rock House Valley sink,
With the same trails leading to it
   Where the deer come down to drink.

There's the same old rugged gorge below
   With the river roaring through,
Where we've all spent many happy hours
   While fishing there with you.

Often, when at Chimney's camp site
   Where the red men long ago
Painted on the rocks above it
   Characters but red men know.

When the day was slowly dying
   Resting by the campfire's glow
We have talked of these same symbols
   Relics of a long ago.

Dear old boy, these trails still call us
    When the autumn time is here
Call us to the trails we traveled
    At the hunting time each year.

We shall always heed the summons,
    Just the same as we used to do,
'Till we're called to take the long trail
    O'er the great divide to you.

            —J. H. JORDAN,
            Bakersfield, California.

Many fine venison steaks and roasts were enjoyed, and the manner in which the game was dressed and cared for made it prime eating. A couple of flour sacks of deer jerky were usually prepared, and a few pieces stuck in a jacket pocket made the stomach more comfortable on many a long ride. Jerky is made by cutting meat in long, narrow strips, and cutting across the grain to make it more tender. Plenty of salt and pepper was used, the pepper being used primarily to keep the flies off. These strips were hung over a wire or cord until dried, and then stored so the air could freely circulate through it. Besides being carried as a snack, a fine gravy and delicious stew were made from either deer or beef jerky.

Often the deer season would end while the cattle were being pushed out through the low country. If a storm hit about the same time, the deer were forced to migrate from the high country. Sometimes the cowboys happened across a dozen or so big bucks, who would just stand and watch them as if they knew perfectly well the season had closed.

The weather at this time of year can change overnight — from sunshine and brilliant fall colors among the quaking aspen and oaks to a blanket of snow on the ground and a howling wind. Camping out is not much fun in rough weather, so special haste was made to get the stragglers down the trail and onto the home ranches.

As the cattle drifted down from the plateau, Stanley Smith usually opened a gate to one of his fields along Highway 178. Every few days, after a fairly large bunch of cattle had collected there, the other cattlemen cut out their stock and took them on to their ranches. A few hurried trips were made back to the mountains to "cut tracks." This was accomplished by riding enough of the country to determine, by recent tracks, if any cattle had been left behind. They would track down those cattle which, for some reason, had not been chased out by foul weather.

The cattleman's life was not all a bed of roses. A person had to be fitted for this type of work or he would not stay with it. The cattle business has often been said to be more than just a business, but a way of life. This was certainly so with the South Forkers. There were a lot of hot, dusty rides. Cowboys, at times in the desert, got so dry they could not even talk. Water holes were few and far between, and tradition kept them from carrying a water bag or canteen. On fall trips they almost froze to death, as there was no way to wear enough clothes to keep warm and still be able to work on horseback.

These cattlemen regretted seeing more of the back country opened up each year. The concept of "Multiple Use" was good, and the Forest Service was wisely practicing it. The thousands of people who enjoyed the Kern Plateau were also entitled to this wonderful experience of camping in the high country, but to some the peace and quiet were gone.

Jim Robertson and Bill Alexander spent fifty years in these mountains, during which time almost nothing changed. Stanley Smith and Marvin Powers rode the mountain ridges and meadows for close to seventy years, having gone to the high country as children in the late 1800's.

These old-timers were not anti-social. But it was hard for them to get used to lining out a bunch of cattle down a trail and having them all come back at you after hearing the roar of a trail bike. Having to untangle a Honda-shy bronc from a bunch of small lodgepole pines made a man wonder if he was not born fifty years too late.

Bill Alexander and Marvin Powers had passed on by 1970. Jim Robertson, over ninety years old, would sit in his home at Weldon and look out over the meadows that used to be dotted with his cattle. Maybe he dreamed of the mountain ridges and canyons he rode for so many years.

In this year, only Stanley Smith remained active in the cattle business, riding and attending to ranch work each day. He gave no thought to retirement. He asked only to be able to work his stock until his last day. During his lifetime he and the other cattlemen of the South Fork went through many trials together, such as grasshopper infestation, screw worms after calf branding, and hard winters. Now, he found himself faced with the almost impossible task of running a cow outfit in the face of high operating expenses and higher taxes.

Although another generation of the Alexanders and Smiths are carrying on the traditions of the three previous generations, the day that Stanley stops riding will mark the end of a special era of Kern County history. These hardy pioneers had put the beef on the nation's table. While not asking for Government subsidies— nor anything else unearned, they were only seeking to support their families and ride the range they all loved.

XIII A. Brown Ranch

A VITAL part of the South Fork economy for the better part of the past century has been that contributed by the A. Brown Ranch at Weldon. With the headquarters located one mile west of the South Fork School on Highway 178, the Company holdings boasted some fourteen thousand acres. About half of this was located in the high country, with the remainder on the Valley floor. This was cut by about three thousand acres in the 1950's when the Corps of Engineers took the west end of the South Fork holdings to use as part of the reservoir for Lake Isabella.

For many years, the A. Brown Store at Weldon was the home of the local bank, post office, boarding house and a country store. What the store didn't carry in merchandise could be ordered via the railroad to Caliente. In the 1880's it also housed the only place where you could get a drink of hard liquor between Isabella, then Barton's Junction, twelve miles to the west, and Scodie's, six miles to the east.

Andrew Brown bought the ranch in 1871 from Alexander Forsyth. As the Weldon Post Office had been established at the ranch that same year, it wasn't long before Brown started stocking various necessities. A virtual trading mecca soon developed. Andrew wasn't a newcomer to the mercantile business as he had tried his hand at running a store in Mariposa County, and also at this time had a store in Kernville.

Andy had also raised stock and farmed in Tulare County, and had done more than a little mining. Soon after he came to Kernville in the middle 1860's he was given the responsibility of being foreman of the Sumner quartz mill.

He was unable to stay away from the store business long though, and in 1869 he bought a brick store building from Kitteredge & Co. in Kernville. Just north of this store he built a home for his wife, the former Alice M. Sumner, whom he married in 1873. It was in this stately home he reared his two children, M. Elizabeth, who later married Dr. Edward M. Pallette of Los Angeles, and P. Sumner, or Summy, as many of his friends called him.

Andy never lived on his South Fork property, but drove over from Kernville when the need arose. Frank Apalatea, who was then just a young lad, tells of seeing Andy Brown's buggy round the turn just west of the ranch. He would happily anticipate a day of going over the vast South Fork holdings with Mr. Brown, as his standing job on these occasions was to ride along in the buggy and open all the gates. Frank was eleven years old when he first ran

The A. Brown Company headquarters at Weldon as seen from the hill behind the ranch. This picture was taken during a snowstorm about 1900. Highway 178 runs through the center of the cluster of buildings. The blacksmith shop at far right and the old store building in the center are almost covered by the trees. At far left is the flour mill.

away from his home on the Piutes and was given a job as chore boy on the A. Brown Ranch. Even in Andy's absence the diversified business operations functioned smoothly. This was undoubtedly due to his keen foresight of the character of his fellow men, and choice of only the most dependable to act in his stead.

Of his many trusted foremen on the ranch, one of the first was John Beaty, who first secured this position in 1884 and held it for many years. In those days a good foreman was getting $45.00 per month plus board and room. Billy Durward, who came to the Kern River in 1879, and for whom Durrwood (incorrect spelling) Meadow and Durrwood Creek north of Kernville were named, was also entrusted with this job of foreman for quite a few years.

It was Rebecca, Billy's sister, who married the pioneer David Alexander, and their son, A. J. or "Art" was one who held this position of foreman the longest. "Art" Alexander was foreman of the farming operation for thirty years, ending in 1937. He then went into business for himself at Onyx.

Other foremen were young Bill Kissack and Bev Robinson. Some of the later foremen were John Gobler and Bob Whitlock who, along with their responsibilities, also contributed a great deal not only to the ranch operation, but also to the community life as a whole.

The cattle raising operation of the ranch was usually delegated to another foreman, and here again such well known names as Bob

Pruitt, Johnny Johnson and Charlie Andress are outstanding. These cow bosses were men who not only knew cattle, horses and every foot of the range, but they also knew men, and were highly respected for their willingness to take their share of the longest and hardest rides.

Another phase of the business on this South Fork ranch was the flour mill. This was built in 1878 and was first powered by a water wheel. About ten years later it was changed to steam power. Many Indians were employed at $1.00 per day to cut cottonwood in the river-bottoms to feed the unceasing appetite of this hungry monster. The flour manufactured by this mill was not only sold locally, but was also shipped out of the Valley. One of the last to be in charge of the mill operation was Therman Short.

The A. Brown store which for many years included the Post Office and bar, was operated on a most fascinating basis. The storekeeper

Andy Brown, pioneer businessman of the Kern River Valley. Taken in 1900.

would grant money to local residents for various reasons. In the daily ledger kept by the storekeeper for the year 1886, and 1887, can be found such entries as Ben Chinaman Pole Tax $3.00. Ben was the ranch cook at this time, at $25.00 per month. Another entry lists the fact that Heo Bon, a Chinese in Kernville, was paid $100.00 from China Joe's account. What this then large sum represented is anybody's guess. It could have been a payment on a loan made to secure passage to America, a gambling debt, as these Chinese loved to gamble, or who knows what! On these same ledgers other transactions were listed, such as hay bought locally and listed at $5.00 per load or ton, and $75.00 per stack. The average stack was estimated at fifteen tons. In addition, payment was made at $1.00 per load for hauling hay for the ranch with their own teams.

One ledger noted that N. P. Petersen received $105.00 for heading grain for Jesus

Billy Durward, known to most of the South Forkers as Uncle Billy.

A. J. Alexander and his wife, Helen. Alexander was ranch foreman for A. Brown for thirty years.

Miranda, who had the ranch just half a mile west of where the short-cut crosses the South Fork. Jesus (pronounced Hay-soose) was a descendant of one of the early Mexican families that had settled in Los Angeles in the 1700's. As legend has it, Jesus may have charged too much at Brown's Store and left his bill unpaid, for the A. Brown Co. later acquired his ranch.

Not one to take advantage of his neighbors, Andy waited many years to clear some of his accounts. Most of the ranchers settled up once a year, at harvest time, or when they sold beef or hogs. There was not nearly as much red tape to money transactions in those days, and many times just a verbal agreement was all that was necessary. As the saying went "A man's word was as good as his bond."

Credit was then as tricky as it is today, and a few would let it become their downfall. This was especially true when it came to charging liquid refreshments. One who reportedly let his appetite run away with him was Bill Nicoll, who apparently lost his ranch to A. Brown primarily due to an unpaid whiskey bill.

The bar of the A. Brown Co. did a thriving business in the 1870's and 1880's, but was discontinued during the 1890's. Entries in the ledgers listed a drink of whiskey at 13c, or several drinks at 25c or 35c. The price of a flask (probably half a pint), was 25c, and a pint was 50c. A quart jug of whiskey was $1.00, whereas a jug of sour mash was listed at $1.50. Whiskey by the half-gallon was listed at $2.00, and one gent paid $8.00 for two gallons of the hard stuff.

Men working on the ranch received room and board and generally wages of $1.00 per day

The A. Brown Store at Weldon pictured in later years. In 1916 the top floor was used by the South Fork Recreation Club to hold their dances. On the left is the cookhouse.

in the 1880's and 1890's. Those who had a family to support must have found it hard to make ends meet. Many had gardens, chickens and a milk cow, and also a good rifle. Anything was meat, from rabbit to deer, and sometimes a long-eared calf. The following prices are listed for staple groceries: Eggs, 25c per dozen; potatoes, 2c per pound; flour, $3.00 per 100 pounds, or a barrel for $5.50; rice, 10c per pound; tea, 50c per pound; coffee, 7c per pound; salt, 25c per pound; sugar, 10c per pound; and bacon, 12c per pound. Other merchandise was priced accordingly. A pair of overalls cost $1.00, shirts were $1.00, $1.25 and $2.25, depending on how fancy you wanted them, and shoes were $1.50 or $2.00 per pair. Quite a few of the white settlers and Indians made their own clothes. One entry listed 12 yards of blue denim at $2.16, and another page indicated the sale of 12 yards of calico for $1.00.

As a trip to Doctor Johnson involved a three hour drive to Kernville, most of the pioneers doctored themselves. For this the ledgers showed the following entries: One bottle Safe Cure $1.25; half-gallon castor oil $1.25; soothing syrup $1.25; one porous plaster 25c; one bottle Sarsaparilla $1.00; one bottle Cherry Pectoral $1.00; and an entry of 25¢ for a bottle of pills.

92

Luxuries were few, but once in a while an entry of one silk handkerchief at $1.25, or 2½ pounds of fancy candy at $1.25, or $3.75 for a hat, would show up among the sales.

Separate entries were made in the day books for each of the two sheep camps when they picked up their supplies and their payrolls. Wages as a rule seemed a little lower for herding sheep than cattle, as Stephen Miranda's salary was listed at $25.00 per month which, of course, also included board.

The same ledgers listed separate enterprises on the ranch such as the blacksmith shop. (Which did a good business.) Such pioneer smiths as Jack Fletcher, Peter Brady, and Henry B. True sent a constant battery of echoes bouncing from anvil to the rocky hillside. Prices fluctuated greatly on blacksmithing. H. B. True may have been slightly high, as Henry Wirth said "he charged a dollar to come in and two to get out" on top of the work he did.

Many of the stories that are told of happenings on the A. Brown Ranch are humorous. One instance is the day China Sam either got too much heat from the kitchen stove, or too much whiskey, and really went on a tear. He was holed up in the kitchen, and was taking pot shots with his rifle at everyone who showed up in the yard. Jim Robertson and a few of the

The flour mill, with a capacity of 15 barrels a day, was built in 1878 and was still standing in 1970. The two low buildings on the left were used as grain warehouses and were always filled to overflowing. Building on right corner of picture is the ranch slaughterhouse, used in later years.

The second story of the mill housed a Gray's patented flour dresser. The flour produced here was of the finest quality and in the 1880's sold for $3.00 per 100 pounds, or a barrel for $5.50.

How the A. Brown Ranch headquarters looked from what is now Highway 178, in horse and buggy days.

other ranch hands got their rifles and kept him pinned down while someone rode to get Charley Taylor, who was Andy's right hand man for so many years.

When Charley arrived he chided the boys for making so much out of nothing, and stated that Sam was okay and he would have a talk with him. He called out to the cook, and started toward the cookhouse, when the Oriental placed either a lucky or well aimed shot in the dust between Taylor's boots, causing him to set a record in high jumps. Turning around in midair, he ran out from under his hat. The cook

finally broke for the bunkhouse and, as he ran full speed through the door, collided with a luckless ranch hand, knocking him half-way under a bed. Happily, they finally got Sam tied up and cooled down without anyone getting seriously hurt.

At the ranch some of the most daring tricks were pulled by Smiley Ramos to amuse his fellow workers. A tough stunt to repeat was to

China Sam poses with his pet bobcat behind the Weldon Store. When the cat disappeared some of the boys claimed he was used in the stew.

93

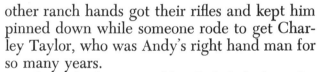

Stevens, the miller, stands on the left with unidentified ranch worker. The mill ran all year except for two weeks when Stevens went on vacation. Photo taken about 1910.

sneak up behind a bronc who was known to be a kicker while it was tied to the hitching rail and dozing in the sun. He would quickly and quietly grab the bronc by the hind feet just above the hooves. Smiley never missed, as far as we know, but you're not allowed to miss in a game such as this.

There was also the occasion in later years when A. J. Alexander, then the cow boss, while watching the packer, Brock Cole, pack the mules for a mountain trip, decided there was too much bedding for the seven men who had left that day to take cattle to Manter Meadow in the high country. The men didn't find out until late that night, when they got ready to turn in, that they were all short on bedding. To make matters worse, it was one of the coldest trips that year, with the wind blowing every night. All the hands slept outside, so you can imagine the cursing and grumbling that went on. Almost to a man, they stated that when they got back to Weldon they would tell Mr. Alexander just what they thought of his meddling.

This was mostly talk though, as there were plenty of men looking for jobs in those days, and a shortage of bed clothes wasn't enough to risk jeopardizing one's job. One young cowboy didn't realize this, though, and as he happened to be the first one off the mountain, he marched right up to A. J. and told him that he had better keep his hands off his bedroll in the future. Alexander's response to this impulsive young man was, "If you don't like it, there's the road," which meant to pack your gear, draw your pay and move out. The cowboy later found out that none of the hands really intended to affront the boss about beds, at least not in such a forthright manner.

The old ranch buildings are falling down one by one, or have reached the point where they have to be taken down for reasons of safety.

The last of the old buildings to remain standing were the blacksmith's shop, the flour mill, and the store building. Time and the elements have made serious inroads on these structures, and it will be only a matter of time until they too, are only memories.

XIV Piutes

O N THE west end of the A. Brown holdings, below the old store, were the H. T. Miller, H. D. Stramler ranches, and just before the Kernville short-cut road, the Charles S. Collins place. All three of these ranches had been bought by Andy Brown in the early days, but in 1893 he had rented the Collins place to William Durward, one of his early ranch foremen. In the year mentioned above, David Alexander brought his family from Scotland to live with his brother-in-law, Durward. In 1910 Brown sold the Collins Ranch to Durward; then in 1918 David's youngest son, Jim, bought the ranch. At this same time he secured a permit from the Forest Service to run cattle on the Piute Mountains. Then Jim moved his family to San Jose, selling the ranch to his brother, Art, and Willy Kneal.

In 1936, Glen, Jim's son, moved back to the Valley and went to work for his uncle Art at Onyx. In 1950 he bought back the old home place. In 1970, Glen, his wife Francis, and their family were still living on the ranch and taking their cattle up the Dry Meadow Trail into the Piutes.

The Dry Meadow Trail was in use as early as 1900, and many of the Piute Miners rode down this old trail to get supplies at the A. Brown store. Although the Piute Mountains are more or less a world all their own, they tie in closely to the South Fork, as much of the northeast part of the Piutes is a tributary to the South Fork, and many of the first miners in the Piutes later came to the South Fork to raise their families.

The byways that skirt this mountain plateau are the Bodfish-Havilah Road on the west, Walker Basin Loop on the south, and the Kelso Valley Road along the eastern extremities. In the 1860's the Kelso Valley Road was the main thoroughfare between Los Angeles and the Kern River mines.

The first road to the Piutes was the Old Bull Road up St. John Ridge. This road was too steep for anything but oxen to navigate, so the Rabbit Foot Road was built up the creek just north of where the Harris Grade is now. The Harris Grade, built in the 1930's, is the main route used to the Piute area. The Saddle Springs Road which fights its way up the western slopes from the Havilah-Bodfish summit is passable but rough, at best.

Down the south side of the mountain are the Buxton Mill Road and the Geringer Grade, neither of which are used much today.

Little physical evidence remains of the ghost town called Claraville, once the home of hundreds of miners. In the winter those miners moved down into Kelso Valley into Sageland. Claraville, named after Clara Munchton — daughter of an early Piute miner—was founded in 1865 when a group of prospectors discovered workable placer gold in the creeks near Landers Meadow.

Accorded the honor of making this first strike was Robert Palmer, Sr. He was no newcomer to mining, as the death of his father in Kentucky forced him to work in the mines at the age of eleven. In 1850 he joined an expedition bound for California. The journey west was made on horseback, with belongings being carried on pack horses. They had none of the protection afforded them that those traveling with covered wagons had, and in one of the several running battles with plains Indians, Palmer was hit in the arm by an Indian arrow— a wound that bothered him the rest of his life.

On arriving in California, Palmer first stopped at Hangtown. After ten years of mining this area, he left for Kernville. Even this

Five children of Robert Palmer Jr., are *left to right*, Evelyn, Virginia, "Buz", Hester and Marguerite—in 1923.

Refugia Williams.

Patriarch of the South Fork, Robert Palmer Jr.

early town was too crowded so he started working such places as the Piute Mountains. It was to the Piutes that he took his bride, the former Rose Glennon, in 1866. Their son, Robert, was the first white child born on the Mountain.

Robert Jr. told how his father had him, at the age of eight, carry gold they were taking to Havilah on his horse. Young Palmer would ride off in the brush a ways and parallel the trail that the rest of the family were traveling. Hold-up men worked those mountain trails quite regularly, and several times they were held up. Each time, though, the elder Palmer told the bandits that they didn't have any gold and were just going into Havilah to try and get some groceries on credit. A search proved he was telling the truth and, although robberies were common, the Palmers never lost one cent in transporting their hard earned wealth off the mountain.

A. D. C. McKay, also known as "Alphabet" McKay.

McKay's place at Paris-Loraine.

In 1876, Robert Sr. moved his family to Hot Springs Valley. With a brood of children that finally numbered twelve, Palmer wanted a school close by, and so he built one. The teacher was paid by private subscription until, in 1883, it became a public school. In 1870 this school still stood, just below the Auxiliary Dam, about a quarter of a mile north of where it was originally built. His desire was for all the children to be educated. A fortunate recipient of this education was Robert Jr., who became the local judge, a position he held for many years.

Palmer's partner in this first mining venture was Wade Hampton Williams, nicknamed "Hamp." Hamp came to California in the early 1850's in the wagon train of Moses B. Hart. After a few years of mining the Piutes, he married an orphan Indian girl known as Refugio. They raised their family of three girls and one boy, Hamp Jr., in Kelso Valley. Of the many mines Hamp located, the most famous was the Joe Walker Mine in Walker's Basin, which he sold for $2,000 soon after discovery. Later a ten day cleanup in the mine netted around $10,000, and in the seven years of production it netted about $600,000. He also located the Gold Peak and Cowboy Mines in Stud Horse Canyon, near Caliente. Hamp Jr., following his Dad's footsteps, discovered the Kelly silver mine near Randsburg.

A daughter, Annie, married Earl McKay. Earl's father, Alexander Daniel Chester McKay, better known as A.D.C. McKay, was also one of the early miners on the Mountain. One of the best known of the mines that he located was the Burning Moscow, but he will be best remembered as starting the gold and silver boom in Caliente Canyon in the early 1860's. This enterprising Scotsman married an Indian native and raised a sizable family. McKay's Hotel and Store at Loraine, known as Paris until 1912, was a popular spot in early Kern County, and many a passenger on the horse drawn stage from Caliente to Bright's Store on the Piutes sat down to a hearty meal served at McKay's Hotel, cooked "fit for a king" by a Chinese cook.

One of the merchants of Claraville in the 1860's was Jeremiah Robinson, born in 1818 in Kentucky. He and his wife, Mary, had migrated from Texas to the gold fields. They arrived in what was later Kern County in 1859, when their first son, Bev, was only six months old. The Robinsons first operated a boarding house on Poso Creek, and it was here that their second son, Jerry, was born in 1861. Their third son, Robert E. Lee, was born after they had moved to Havilah. Later Jeremiah oper-

Robert E. Lee and Lydia Robinson.

family to Kernville. Again she managed to support her family by washing and cooking for the miners. Grandmother Robinson, as she came to be known, lived in Kernville until her death in 1929. Her sons also raised families there. Many descendants still lived in the Valley in 1970.

The magic of the Piutes held many in its grasp down through the years. Francisco Apalatea, called Pancho by many of the Valley residents, was one of these. Pancho came to the Piutes in 1873, bringing with him three children from his first wife whom death claimed in Kelso in 1874. He then married Mary Butterbredt, daughter of Frederick Butterbredt, an early Piute miner. Before her death, Mary added another six children to his family. His last wife, Rosie Rice, bore him an additional eight children, for a total of seventeen. These children have left a host of descendants in the Kern River Valley.

Pancho, known as the dean of the prospectors, located many mines on the Piute Mountains. Some of these mines were the Shoemaker, Cast Iron, McKinley, and the Bryn, the last being his most profitable one. It was the sale of the Bryn Mine in 1905 that gave him the capital to purchase a ranch from Andy Brown, now the present site of Kernville. This ranch was homesteaded in 1896 by Albia Curliss. Curliss also built the house which was called the Apalatea house, and later the old Burlando

ated a butcher shop in Claraville. It was in this pioneer town that Robinson met his untimely death by a pistol shot. He was buried at the edge of Claraville in one of the many unmarked graves that now dot the area.

Mary Robinson and her three small boys moved back to Havilah. It was desperately hard for a mother of three to make a living, but with a few hogs and chickens, supplemented by washing clothes, which she did for the miners, she managed. In the early part of 1870 some of the County officials decided it would be better if the boys were taken and distributed to other families. Maybe they meant well, but Mrs. Robinson, hearing what the County had planned, moved out during the night. Lack of transportation didn't bother her. She just packed up what they could carry on their backs and, driving her hogs in front of her, took her

Robinson Family. *Back row, left to right,* Ed, Edna (Mother), Anna, Jerry, Bev. Sr. holding John; *front row,* Mary, Bev. Jr., Lizzy, and Bill.

house—as Pancho sold the ranch to one of his sons-in-law, Matt Burlando. Some of those born in this old house were Al Apalatea, Billie Burlando, and Bobby Robinson. Dr. Smith, who practiced for many years in the Kern River Valley, told of one delivery he made in a tent used as sleeping quarters behind the house. There were too many children in the house to use it for a delivery room. When the time came they found that a hen was getting ready to lay an egg on the bed. Dr. Smith said that the prospective mother insisted on waiting until the hen had laid the egg, and when she ran cackling into the yard, the mother went in and delivered.

Pancho Apalatea wasn't content to live away from the Piutes and, after selling the ranch to his son-in-law, he headed back for the mountains. One of his discoveries this time was the Apalatea Mine.

Pancho milled most of his ore by the most primitive methods. Most of his mines were too far from any mill to make hauling ore profitable. Many times he would drag the ore downhill from the claim on a cow hide. After breaking the rock up to the size of a fist, he would throw it into an arrastra. The arrastra is a round, shallow pit with the bottom and foothigh sides made of closely fitted rock. A post set in the middle held one end of a pole, to which was fastened a drag rock. A little mercury was usually added to the mixture. As the pole was pulled around, the ore was crushed by the drag rock. A blindfolded mule usually furnished the power, but sometimes Pancho would give a couple of the kids a short shift if they misbehaved. You can well imagine that they had little use for this type of exercise.

Apalatea would haul the bullion on a spring wagon pulled by a team of mules through Kelso, spending the first night at Cinco. The next day he moved on to Mojave, where he shipped the gold.

Pancho, like many of the Piute miners, did most of his shopping at the A. Brown Store in Weldon, although Scodies at Onyx and McKay's Store at Loraine were used too. Most often he would pay his store bill only once or twice a year, as did many ranchers and miners throughout the Valley. In Pancho's declining years he came to live with his daughter, Lupie Burlando. Although he was very weak and al-

Francisco Apalatea and his first wife, taken in Porterville in 1872.

most blind, he still had gold fever and would sneak away from the house to prospect up Bull Run Creek for that last big strike. One evening he disappeared, and a search failed to turn him up. The next morning he was found crawling through the brush, completely exhausted, but still sure, if he could get up on that last ridge, he would make that last big strike. Although Pancho did not leave much of monetary value, he left a heritage, long to be remembered.

Whenever the conversation gets around to old time miners, Otto Leibel is mentioned. He and his partner, Ward Olds, worked some of the richest claims in the Piute Mountains. One

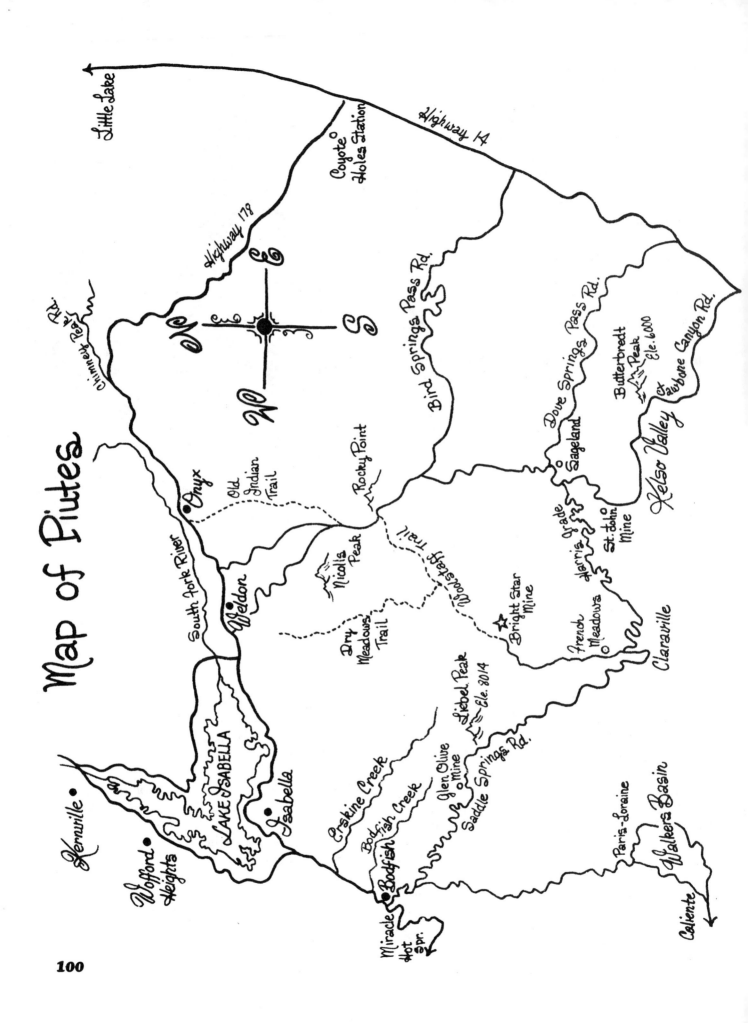

Map of Piutes

Little Lake

Highway 14

Coyote Holes Station

Highway 178

Chimney Peak Rd.

Onyx

South Fork River

Old Indian Trail

Rocky Point

Bill Springs Pass Rd.

Dove Springs Pass Rd.

Butterbredt Peak Ele. 6000

Jawbone Canyon Rd.

Kelso Valley

Sageland

Harris Grade

St. John Mine

Nicolls Peak

Woolstead Trail

Bright Star Mine

Dry Meadows Trail

Weldon

French Meadows

Claraville

Liebel Peak Ele. 8014

Erskine Creek

Bodfish Creek

Glen Olive Mine

Saddle Springs Rd.

Paris-Loraine

Walkers Basin

Kernville

Wofford Heights

Lake Isabella

Isabella

Bodfish

Miracle Hot Spr.

Caliente

100

Frederick Butterbredt came to the Kern River country in the early 1850's.

Mary Butterbredt, her aunt. As Emma put it, she "hid real good," and it was four days until Otto found her and convinced her to come home with him.

Life was pretty rugged on the Piutes in the early 1900's. The town of Claraville had faded away and the closest settlement with a store was Paris, or Loraine, as it is now called. Trips were made off the mountain on foot by Otto and the other miners to A.D.C. McKay's store and saloon at Paris-Loraine. Occasionally these miners, not having seen the bright lights for many weeks, would extend the two day trip to four or five days. In such cases Emma would patiently wait, knowing full well what had happened. Supplies were backpacked up the mountain. This was a rough trip, especially in the winter, and on one of these trips George Ross, a Piute miner, became lost in a snowstorm while returning from McKay's, and froze to death.

Sometimes their supplies were packed in from A. Brown's Store at Weldon by Pat Brady. With the earnings made on several of his mines, Otto bought a ranch in the upper end of Erskine Creek Canyon.

When the Liebels moved off the Mountain they had only one child, although their family

Otto and Emma Leibel and two of their grandchildren.

of their best claims was the Jeannette, where they withdrew a small fortune in gold. Marriageable women were few and far between in the early 1900's on the Piutes and neighboring Kelso Valley, so it seemed only fair that when Otto picked Emma Reich as his bride that he should lend Emma's stepfather, Fred Butterbredt, $500 with no definite time set for repayment.

The day Otto and Emma got married is a day still to be remembered. After the ceremony Otto and his friends staged a drawn out drinking party. By the time it was ten hours old, Emma began to have misgivings. She caught a big white horse and separated herself from the wedding party by riding to the St. John Mine. Her story fell on the sympathetic ear of finally numbered four boys and three girls. This was George, a baby at the time. Although Mrs. Liebel disagreed with him, George claims that the trip down the mountain in 1905 was made with him in a barley sack.

Otto Liebel, like many men stuck in mining camps, was brilliant, and undoubtedly could have excelled in many other fields. But the gold fever stayed with him all his life and, except for the time spent on the ranch at Erskine Creek, he could usually be found roaming the hills seeking another big strike.

Most of the Liebel boys, although following other occupations than mining, inherited this love for prospecting. They often would talk for hours about the time spent trying to trace down a rich piece of float someone had picked up. One such piece of ore, shot through with gold, was found by their great-grandfather, Fred Butterbredt, which prompted the boys to cover many miles of the mountains that they loved. Also part of the Piute story are many more mining families such as John and Mattie Moreland, who spent most of their lives on the Mountain.

Scattered over the Piute Mountains are the remains of several sawmills. The first of these mills was brought over from Greenhorn and set up just west of French Meadow. The mill was operated in 1866 by Ashe and Cross in Section T28S, R34E and later moved to the Bright Star Mine in Section 8. It remained there during the life of that mine. Later it was moved to Mace Meadow to supply lumber for several mines in that vicinity. The main use of the lumber from these early mills centered around mining. The Piute Sawmill was established in 1933 just below French Meadow by the Horn Brothers. Timber was harvested until 1953, at which time the mill closed down. Between 1942 and 1952, the B & C Mill was set up for the clear cut of two sections of private land near Mace Meadow. The Buxton Mill was the last to operate on the Piutes, and ran until the 1960's.

Another of the old-time cowboys who ran cattle on the Piutes was Nick Williams. Named Nicholas James Williams, he held the honor of being the first white child born in newly formed Kern County. The year was 1866. His parents raised him in and around Walker's Basin. In 1873 Nick's Dad bought a few head of cattle

Nick Williams, first white child born in Kern County, taken when he was about 81.

from Dan Walser and the first calf, a line-back heifer, was given to Nick. This started him in the cattle business, which he followed the rest of his life.

In 1890 he married Alice Yates. Alice was born in Salem, Massachusetts, having been brought to the Valley as a small girl via Lynn's Valley. Alice was one of the finest women riders in the county and, before her marriage to Nick, had run her mother's cattle in the Wagy Flat area. Four children were born to Nick and Alice: Mary Alice, Virginia Ann, Lyman Elwood and Beatrix. Three years after the birth of Beatrix, Alice passed away—leaving Nick with four children under eight years of age. In 1900, Nick married Mae McClure, and an additional eight daughters were born to this union.

Nick was known for his uncanny ability to handle mean horses with a minimum of trouble, especially when it came to shoeing or doctoring. Although he and his family lived in Walker's Basin, he spent much of his life on the Piute Mountains. In the late 1900's Nick took a contract to gather cattle for Pete McQuirk. Many of these cattle which ran on the Piutes were as wild as March hares, as they saw man

Charley Brown, Piute miner.

only about once a year. This job called for good cowboys and fast horses. For this particular gathering, Nick also used several good dogs and a big, strong "calreste"—an animal used to help lead wild cattle out of the hills.

Nick's calreste, named Lucky, was a roan Durham steer that weighed nearly 2,000 pounds. He had a wide strap around his neck. After the wildest cattle had been stopped with dogs or the cowboys' long rawhide reata, they were tied to a tree overnight. The next morning Lucky was led to the spot and, after the wild cow was tied to the strap around his neck, Lucky did the rest. He either led or dragged his charge home, and waited in the corral until released from his charge.

Other top-notch cowboys who worked in this country with Nick were Jim Polkinhorn, Johnny Weldon, and Jim Palmer, who were the last of the old time "brush poppers." The country didn't get too rough or the cattle too wild for these boys. Nick acquired quite a bit of property on top of Piute, part of which in later

years was turned into a Scout ranch named "Camp Nick Williams."

One of Nick's camps on the Piutes was called "the onion patch" because of the many wild onions growing around the meadow. About 1900 a miner named Charley Brown settled here, and it soon became known as Brown's Meadow. Charley and a couple of companions named Clinton Brooks and Archie Clapp had tried making their strike in Randsburg and, failing there, worked their way across Kelso Valley, up through French Meadow, and finally stopped at "the onion patch."

Brooks and Clapp did not stay, but Charley did, and took out a claim on Brown's Meadow. During the next ten years he prospected around the Piutes. On Erskine Creek he dug a hole which was called the Bluebird Mine. To the west of Bluebird he dug another which he called Treasury Mine.

Charley made his living by working at the King Solomon Mine and various other places in the area to obtain some cash. He also had a few head of cattle running in Sequoia National Forest. In the early 1900's Charley married, but his wife became sick and died in the cabin he had at the Bluebird Mine. Charley enlisted in the Army and became a First Sergeant in an engineering company. He spent his summers at Brown's Meadow and his winters on property he owned in Walker's Basin.

In 1923, while working on the Doyle Ranch in the South Fork, he fell and was badly injured. He was taken to the hospital in Bakersfield. Permanent disability resulted, and with the cash he was awarded from Workmen's Compensation, he purchased a small Cleveland tractor that he took up on the mountain. The little tractor caused his death in 1929 while he was hauling mine track at the Treasury Mine. A track slipped on a rock; the tractor flipped, pinned Charley underneath, and dragged the mine track over him.

As far as known, Brown had no relatives, and left nothing but a meadow named after him and a host of friends who had visited him on the mountain over the years. They remember vividly his sourdough hot cakes with homemade gooseberry jelly which he offered, along with his friendship, to all who came by. Such was the nature of those who lived on this mountain plateau.

XV Neill Ranch

JUST WEST of the Kernville cut-off road is the ranch that was known for many years as the Taylor place. Originally settled by C. J. E. Taylor, it was purchased in the late 1800's by Robert Neill. Along with the Taylor property, Neill had also bought the Swan and Gray ranches, and by 1900 what was then known as the the Neill Ranch stretched west for over a mile, taking in 840 acres.

In 1934, John, Robert's brother, bought the biggest portion of these holdings, and moved onto the place from his home in the Hot Springs Valley. John's daughter, Dora, had married Alex Silicz, and in 1934 he turned the ranch over to the Silicz family. John immediately contracted with Clare A. Tuttle to build an impressive home on the east end of this property, and also made a gift of it to his son-in-law's family. Alex and Dora had raised a family of three boys and three girls in the Hot Springs Valley, and they all moved to their new home on the South Fork. The family then used this ranch as the headquarters for their cattle operation.

Both Alex and Dora had been born in the Kern River Valley. Alex was born in the old Joseph Caldwell house in Quartzburg, which was the first home built on the Kern River. This old house burned before 1900, but the old rock chimney remained there as a landmark on the flat above the Kernville cemetery for many years.

When Alex was small his father was accidentally shot in a bar in Kernville and never completely recovered. The family moved to Bakersfield where Alex spent his early years working for such pioneer ranches as the Miller and Lux and the Kern County Land Company. In 1908 Alex married the former Dora Neill, and the young couple went into the cattle business with Dora's father, John. At this time the Neill fam-ily had their ranch headquarters at Wagy Flat, where John had lived since 1875 when he came there to work oxen for Mr. Wagy in his sawmill there.

Dora was an accomplished horsewoman; learning the art as a young lady, she was able to keep up with the men as they worked the wild cattle out of the rugged Greenhorn country. In her early days she rode a sidesaddle, making the task even more hazardous.

Two things made the Neill-Silicz cattle operation unusual. The first was the fact that their range was the most inaccessible in the west. Most of it was steep, rocky country covered with almost impenetrable brush fields. The other unusual aspect was that theirs was a year-round range; that is, the cow herd stayed on the range year round, not coming into the home ranch in the winter time.

The Silicz children learned the cattle business early. The two older boys, John and Bud, were the ones who handled most of the work with the wild cattle, but the girls also were counted as experts with stock. They married men who also understood and loved the cattle business.

Eleanor, better known as Sis, married Franky Schneider, who was not only a working cowboy but in 1933 and 1934 was World Champion Bull Rider. In 1935 Schneider was also World Champion Bareback Rider.

Marian, better known as Mernie, married Burel Mulkey, who became World Champion All Around Cowboy. Like Schneider, Mulkey cowboyed before and after his stretch with the rodeo circuit. Burel's name was entered in the Rodeo Hall of Fame in 1968, at which time both he and his wife lived and ran cattle in the Kern River Valley.

Millie, the youngest girl of the Silicz family, married Foster Webb, also a cattleman, and who became the manager of a land bank and production credit unit at Bishop, California.

Doug, the youngest boy, while a topnotch cowboy, came along a little late to get in on much of the working of the wild cattle on the Greenhorn range. However, he had grown up in the cattle business, and in 1970 was cattle foreman for Monroe Brown of Wheatland, in charge of 8,000 head, a position he has held for many years.

The Neill-Silicz range covered the area from what is now Lake Isabella west almost to Bakersfield, with the southern boundary being the Kern River and the northern boundary adjoining Petersen's range. In those early days there were no fences, and once or twice a year the cowboys would have to go into the Glennville country and work back any of the cattle that had drifted off the home range.

It is hard to describe the type of work that goes into getting cattle to market off this kind of range. In other types of cattle operations the cattle become more or less gentle from being driven to and from summer and winter range. The more they come into contact with people, generally the easier they are to handle. Take for instance the case of a four year old steer raised on the Silicz range; the last time he had any dealings with a cowboy might have been when he was roped as a calf out on the range

Alex Silicz, with one of the cow dogs he used to help him work wild cattle on Greenhorn Mountain.

three years previously, and branded. He hadn't learned any gentle bovine ways from his mother, as the cows were even wilder than the steers. The calves would learn early in life the ways of the wild bunch.

One favorite trick was to head for the thickest brush patch in the vicinity. If the cowboy had anticipated the moves, the steer would find the path blocked by a horse and rider. He might be turned once, but more commonly he would charge anything or anyone in his way. He was furious as a caged tiger, and with bayonet-sharp horns would hook anything out of his way. An 800 pound steer has the power to raise a horse and rider clear off the ground, but the horses ridden on Greenhorn were seldom hooked. Raised on the range, they were as much at home in that steep, rocky country as the cattle. Horses could anticipate the move of the animal being pursued, and the rider had better have a deep seat in the saddle at all times if he didn't want to be left sitting on the ground at the mercy of the flashing horns.

The success of a roundup depends tremendously on good horses. In the thick brush many times a mountain-wise horse will follow the trail of a wild cow by the scent alone when the rider is unable to pick up any tracks on the ground. Once a cowboy has a rope on a steer's head and they are jerked to a stop, almost without fail they turn and charge. If there is another man handy he will hurry to get a rope on the hind feet. This type of team roping cannot be compared with that seen in a rodeo

Dora Silicz worked cattle on the rugged slopes of Greenhorn Mountain, riding a sidesaddle in her younger days. In the background is the old Edison Flume.

Earl McKay—a good cowhand in any man's country.

arena as all the breaks are against the ropers. Uneven ground, steep country, or having only a forty-foot opening in which to work might make getting the animal roped seem next to impossible. But these oldtimers seldom missed.

Once the animal is on the ground a short rope is tied to his horns, and he is tied to a tree to think things over for a while. It is surprising how much being tied to an oak tree overnight does for their disposition. Getting these huge animals up against a tree was a pretty big chore even for two men, but what seems unbelievable is that more times than not, these brush poppers worked alone.

One of the best of these oldtimers was Earl McKay, an outstanding tracker, partly due to his Indian blood and partly from years of training, working cattle from Old Mexico to California. Earl had tracked humans as well as animals while with the Border Patrol, and when he got on the track, his quarry seldom got away.

A dead shot with a rifle, Earl once killed four deer with four shots. Not one to brag about his accomplishments, Earl explained, "there weren't hardly any deer that year. I had hunted almost a month and seen nothing so when I jumped that bunch I had to get them. I only had four shells for my 30-30 and I killed a deer with each shot except for the last one. I didn't hit him right and had to finish him off with my knife." This rifle he used for so many years became like his right hand; he was extremely fast bringing it into play, and seldom missed.

One day the ranch hands got split up after they jumped a good sized bunch of cattle. When they found McKay later in the day, he had seven head tied up in the brush. Earl ex-

plained some of his methods, which were, in turn, used by most of the people who ran wild cattle. The expression "running wild cattle" is misleading, as the cowboys didn't just take out after the first wild cow they saw. Each time careful plans would be made to give the rider the needed advantage to get within roping distance of the animal they were after.

They used all the strategy of a field general and took into account the habits of that individual animal, which in many cases included the route he might take after he was jumped. The cowboy would work into a position where a fairly short burst of speed would put him within roping distance of his quarry. As Earl explained it, for this work he packed a fairly short rope, many times only twenty feet long. He built a horn knot on one end, and when working alone he slipped this over the horn of his saddle. Once the cowboy had the steer roped, the action really started. What happened many times was described as follows by McKay:

"When you got your rope on them they would nearly always turn and charge. This was the best time to put the trip to them as you had plenty of slack in your rope. You wheeled your horse out of the way and let the animal go by, throwing enough slack in your rope to let them get their front feet over it. You jump your horse out the other way and when the horse hits the end of the rope the animal's head is jerked back under him and he usually goes down."

As the cowboy sees the cow go down, he is off his horse immediately. The horse is trained to keep pulling until his rider yells "whoa." Thus the cow is kept down and busy until the man can get in position to tie him with a piggin string (a short rope carried stuck in the belt).

Once on the ground and tied up, the next thing was to try to get him tied to a tree. Being tied to a tree for a few hours gave the wild one a chance to work off much of his excess energy. The rope being tied from the horns to an immovable object made them respond more readily to being led out to the ranch. The head and horns were just plain tender. If watching a tree grow for twenty-four hours didn't bring them to time enough to be handled with a minimum of resistance, forty-eight hours or longer was prescribed.

Many methods were used in the early days to get the beef to the ranch, but the one favored by Neill and Silicz was to tie them to a big, gentle steer who called the ranch home, and he would lead or drag the outlaw home. Neill had two of these steers, and in the old days they were used to bring hundreds of cattle in that had gone wild. Many times cowboys would lead cattle in with their horses and, as has been stated before, the horse seldom was hooked, as they seemed to have eyes in the back of their head. The horse always seemed to be a jump ahead of the cow when she charged. Once a man started leading a wild one in, before long the steer or cow being led would gentle down quickly after they were taken out of familiar country. Many times when they were led into the home corral the animal would be leading on a loose rope right up beside the horse, those big, sharp horns even rubbing the cowboy's leg at times. They seemed to know they had met their match, and submitted to captivity.

Many of the top-notch cowboys were small men. Take McKay, for instance. When you talk about a man tying down seven head of wild cattle by himself, you might think he would be 6-feet 3-inches tall and weigh 200 pounds, but Earl was only 5-feet 5-inches tall and never weighed more than 118 pounds in the days when he punched cows.

Bud Silicz paid Earl the highest compliment possible when he said of him "he was always at the right place at the right time with a fresh horse." Anybody can run a horse to death, but these brush poppers knew how to not only conserve their horse's strength, but were experts in all areas of care for their mounts, from feeding them to the care of their feet and backs. Among the other good cowboys who rode for the Silicz brothers were Marcus Avilsz, Remick Albitre, Arthur Esponda, better known as Chipmunk, and Lee Petersen, whose father and grandfather had also run cattle on the Greenhorn Mountain.

Bud and John Silicz were two of the best in the game. John was known as being one of the best dalley men in the Valley. To dalley, is for a roper to take turns around the horn of his saddle with his rope after he has an animal on the other end. Sometimes the cowboy has

Bob Neill, friend to all who lived on the South Fork.

plenty of time to put on his dallies, but other times they must make their moves with lightning speed or lose the animal altogether. John Silicz demonstrated this speed on many occasions.

He was known to rope horses going by him in a lane, on a dead run, while sitting on his saddle horse. Anyone who has roped much, can tell you, that this is one of the hardest feats a roper can try. As the horse passed, John would make his catch, jerk his slack, and as his horse wheeled in the direction of the departing "tornado," would pile just the right amount of dallies on the saddle horn. Too many would stop the horse too suddenly, either causing his saddle horse to be jerked down, or breaking his rope or saddle rigging. So he whipped just the right number of wraps on the horn and let his rope run a little to make the stop a little less sudden, the smoke fairly flying from the friction caused.

The Bob Neill home, one of the last landmarks of the South Fork Valley's colorful past.

The staircase in the old Neill house as it appeared in 1970. Due to outstanding workmanship and good care over the years, the home remained in excellent condition.

Cattle are still being run in the Greenhorn country but they are gathered off the range every year and there are no more "mossy horned" steers lying in the oak thickets waiting to slip down a hidden draw the first time they catch sight of a cowboy.

The Siliczs sold the ranch to a Dr. Stoops and he, in turn, sold to Dr. Prince. Valley men were retained as foremen and Burel Mulkey held this position for many years. In 1970 Arthur Esponda was running the ranch for the doctor.

A mile further west, on the lower edge of what was the Robert Neill holdings, there appears a large, two-story house. Bob had the home built in the 1890's for his fiancee. The girl died before the marriage and Neill, then forty years old, never married. His sister, Millie, came to live with him, and for years presided as a gracious hostess in the home.

Four of the Neill brothers had arrived in the Valley in 1875, and for a time worked for Evans at his sawmill on Greenhorn Mountain. At this time Evans used oxen in his lumber operation. Their parents, James and Marion Neill, were both natives of Scotland but had settled on Prince Edward's Island.

Bob, the oldest of eight children, was born in 1852. After finishing school he worked on his father's farm until 1872. He then worked a year as a broad-axe man for Swift and Company, to log oak timbers for the Navy shipyards. After a short time at Evans' mill, Bob

hired to the Sumner Mining Company at Kernville as a car-man and later as a fireman. Then he served ten years as clerk and bookkeeper for Andy Brown, Judge Sumner's son-in-law. Most of these years as bookkeeper were spent in the A. Brown Store at Weldon, and his fine penmanship is exhibited in the A. Brown ledgers of the 1880's. Bob had filed on his original homestead in 1889. His brand, RN, could be found on a large herd of Shorthorn Durham cattle. At one time he had over 200 acres of alfalfa under irrigation.

It has been said that Bob Neill and his sister had only kindness for others, and the South Fork residents deeply missed them when they passed away. In 1970 the old Neill home was still being used as a residence. But the house is within the take-line of Lake Isabella. The last time the old home was threatened, permission was acquired to build a levee to hold the lake waters back. Soon only the memories of those who enjoyed the hospitality of the Neills will remain.

XVI Petersen Ranch

Most of the men who came to work the mines in the Kern River Valley remained anonymous, going their itinerant ways and leaving nothing by which their names would be remembered. Some, however, stayed on, going into ranching and other businesses when the mining faded out. They established homes and families. Some of their descendants still live in the Valley. One of those who remained was Niels Peter Petersen, a Dane born in 1841 on the Island of Leso, a possession of Denmark.

N. P. Petersen, as everyone in the Kern River Valley called him, went to sea when he was fourteen years old, shipping out from Copenhagen as a cook on a schooner bound for England. For seven years he followed the sea. In 1862 he landed in San Francisco, and there he enlisted in the United States Navy for one year. Oddly enough, it was this hitch in the Navy that eventually led the Dane to hear the call of the gold fields and later go to work in the Sumner Mine in the Kern River Valley. As it happened, Petersen's first lieutenant was a stockholder in the mine.

Petersen arrived in Kernville in May of 1864. He went to work for Judge Sumner, and for the next nine years lived a miner's life and saved his money. In 1871, Petersen took up land on the South Fork of the Kern River. It was this land that was his most prized possession, as he continued to prosper. In 1873, Petersen bought property and built the Kernville Hotel, which provided food and lodging a little above the usual mining town fare. Besides owning many dwellings in Kernville, the Golden Gate Hotel in Havilah was added to the family holdings.

He married Mrs. Lizzie Annie Swett in 1876. Mrs. Swett brought to the union two small sons by a previous marriage, John and William. She also brought an abounding energy and vast en-

thusiasm for the hotel business. Both the marriage and the business proved fruitful. In due time, three children, Howard, Adeline and Walter, were born to the Petersens.

In 1883 the Kernville Hotel was destroyed by a fire that swept through town. Lost with it were other structures owned by Petersen. A story passed down through the years bears out the fact that N. P. wasn't a man to cry over spilled milk. On the day in 1883 when the fire swept through Kernville, a rider was dispatched to the Petersen Ranch, some twelve

N. P. Petersen, pioneer South Fork rancher. **109**

The Kernville Hotel was one of Petersen's many business ventures.

miles distant, to break the bad news. He found Mr. Petersen and an Indian named Logan, building a flume that was to be used as part of his ditch bringing water from the South Fork. The messenger pulled his lathered horse to a stop and broke the news. N. P.'s only comment was "hand me another board, Logan."

After such a big loss on his town property, N. P. turned more of his energy to the land. In 1888 he constructed another ditch from the river to put more of his land under irrigation. He acquired adjoining land until he had 1,200 acres. This was in addition to two ranches he owned on Greenhorn Mountain. These Greenhorn ranches were used mostly for the summer headquarters of his cattle operation. The NP brand was known throughout Kern County. Never one to pass up an opportunity, Petersen was quick to see that a threshing machine could be a boon to every rancher in the area, so he got one.

It became a custom for the various ranches to pool their manpower at harvest time. Men

and the Petersen thresher moved from ranch to ranch until the work was completed. One of the men who worked on these crews as a lad was Amos Petersen, N. P.'s grandson, and son of Walter Petersen. Amos, like his father and grandfather, continued to ranch and was still running cattle on the South Fork in 1970.

As hard as all the jobs were connected with threshing, it was easy to get men to work on the threshing crew. It may seem unusual, but many of the Indians would quit other jobs when the harvesting season started, and show up at the Petersen ranch ready to go to work. One of the reasons seemed to be the steam whistle that could be heard for miles. This was sounded in the morning when enough steam was built up to start the operation, at noon, and at quitting time. This lure of the whistle, the excitement of the fire-belching steam engine, and the prospect of eating the big meals put out by N. P.'s Chinese cook were always enough to enlist a good sized crew. Men received their board and room and one dollar per day.

110

How men, machine, and animals worked together to accomplish the task is interesting in itself. Earlier in the year grain hay had been cut, raked, and stacked. At the start of the threshing operation a large wagon with an A-frame structure on it was pulled up beside the stacked hay. This wagon was called a hay table. A cable running through a pulley suspended from the A-frame was fastened to a Jackson fork at one end and to a team of horses at the other. The horses supplied the power which activated the Jackson fork, which in turn pulled the hay onto the hay table. Two men pitched hay from the hay table into the threshing machine.

A minimum of ten men was required to operate the thresher. One man worked the Jackson fork, which was a set of six, three-foot curved teeth set in a four-foot hardwood handle. These teeth were sunk into the haystack and the team would supply the power to pull a large quantity of hay off the stack and onto the hay table at the right moment. The fork man would pull a trip rope that caused the fork to release its load at the right spot. There was always a constant danger from this swinging fork and at least one man, Alphy Kneal, had the dubious distinction of surviving after being run through the stomach with one of these three-foot tines. Alphy, an old hand at the game, apparently was just not quick enough *this* time.

One man handled the team that powered the fork, and two additional men were kept busy pitching a steady stream of hay into the stom-

Lizzie Petersen poses with her five children: *In back, left to right, standing,* Howard, Adie and Walter Petersen; *seated, left to right,* John and Bill Swett.

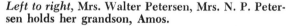

Left to right, Mrs. Walter Petersen, Mrs. N. P. Petersen holds her grandson, Amos.

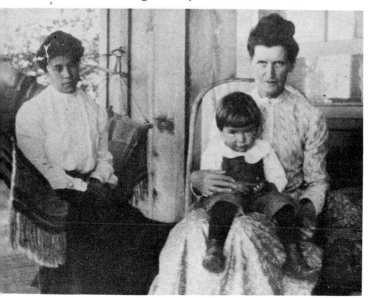

ach of the clattering thresher. Water was hauled in wooden kegs by a wagon, and one man kept the boilers full of water and the machinery oiled. A hot job was keeping the boiler fire stoked with cottonwood, which was cut and hauled from the riverbottom by two more men.

Danger of fire was always present when harvesting. Sparks from the steam engine were a constant hazard. To reduce the fire hazard, the engine was set quite a distance from the hay stack and the thresher was connected to the machine with a long continuous belt. Heavy screen also protected the engine's smokestack. With the right conditions, however, the cry of "Fire" would ring out and everyone would come running and, with water buckets, quickly quench the blaze.

One of the last times anyone tried to use the thresher was on the ranch just west of Mt. Mesa and now under Lake Isabella. This was after N. P. had passed away. Nobody seems to remember exactly how everything was set up. Even Petersen's grandson, Amos, who had seen it operate, was in a quandary. Finally everything seemed to be going fine. A head of steam was building up, and the men were all at their stations. Then it happened. The steam pressure just kept building, and nobody seemed to remember how to make the pressure release work. The whistle shrieked madly. By this time everybody had started backing away from the

111

The Petersen Thresher.

The steam engine that powered the thresher.

steam monster that seemed very much alive. Although nobody can remember who started first, the whole crew broke into a run.

Luckily steam escaped from minor breaks to keep the boiler from blowing and, as the wood in the fire box burned down, things went back to normal. The crew finally was able to struggle through that one last job. It was decided that without N. P. Petersen, Frank Fugitt, or any of the other old-time thresher men, they wouldn't attempt to operate it again. Never again did that magical whistle call the South Forkers to where men toiled like ants and the grain flowed in a golden stream from this old steam threshing machine.

From the ranch just off the Old Short-Cut Road, N. P. ran his various enterprises. Here was located a complete blacksmith shop, barns for his stages and wagons, and corrals for the many head of stock used in his work. It was here also that he maintained a cookhouse staffed by several different Chinese cooks. One who was longest remembered was China Joe, who was an artist with food, especially pastry. Adie, N. P.'s daughter, in reminiscing, tells us a birthday cake this Oriental baked for her when she was a little girl was a work of art. China Joe also baked delicious pies and doughnuts. But all this didn't impress Mr. Petersen, who seemed not to have a sweet tooth, and he accused the cook of "trying to put on airs." He felt that staples such as meat and potatoes were enough.

Many of the local Indians showed up at dinner and were always made welcome. Besides freely sharing his table with his friends, he made a constant round of small loans on the spot with nothing in writing. In those days a man's word was looked on as more binding than the most legal paper a lawyer could conjure up.

Petersen's stage line was also an important part of his diversified business. The main stage that ran from Caliente to Kernville was of the type called the "mud wagon." The main difference between this and the Concord type was that driver and passengers all were on the same level in the mud wagon. The sides had curtains that could be lowered, but in good weather were left rolled up. This conveyance was pulled by four horses.

Best remembered were four white horses used during the first few years of the 1900's. Vick Phillips, who was at this time driving a freight wagon for Charlie Bennett, and who drove this team twice himself, described them as runaways. Petersen's chief driver during this period was a gent whose name has been lost somewhere along the line, described as a "ruddy faced fellow who always got well oiled before he left Caliente." He was a good reinsman, though, and even in his precarious condition he put on a real exhibit of driving skill. On straighter stretches, such as that through Walker's Basin, he would drive full tilt — taking many of the corners on two wheels.

At least once, due to a judgment error and inebriated state, he took one turn too fast and the stage ended on its side in a tangle of frightened horses and passengers. After Vick Phillips, a teamster who was present when the accident occurred, helped the stage driver set the stage on its wheels, it wasn't long before he again had the team running as hard as they could.

Another driver was Tom Gonzales, who many people in the Valley counted as a good friend. Pete Larson, a nephew of N. P., drove the two-horse stage that took the passengers from Isabella to Onyx.

It was on the run from Walker's Basin to Kernville that the last stage robbery in the area took place. As the stage had just reached the Havilah summit, on one of these routine runs, a bold daytime stagecoach holdup occurred. The year was 1896, and the driver was young John Swett, N. P.'s stepson.

Jim Polkinghorn, a young lad working on the McGuirk ranch at Havilah, related the following account of the holdup that made such a lasting impression on him. Just as the stage had reached the Havilah summit, a masked man with a six shooter stepped out of the brush and stopped it. Aboard the stage were two or three men who were experts with shooting irons, but they were helpless in the face of the gun leveled at them. The bandit ordered the driver to hand over the express box, which held the gold and silver. The chest was bolted to the underside of the floor boards. After the box was loosened and fell to the ground, the gunman ordered the driver to be on his way. Later, the empty box was found at some distance from the scene of the holdup. It had been broken

South Fork young people—1896—on the beach in Kernville. *Front row*, Sophie Lowell, Alonzo Gibony, Jessie Andress, Wade Fine; *back row, from left*, May McCray, Cecil Hanning, Lottie Andress, Joe Lowell, August Glade, and Grace Gibony.

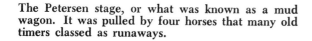

The Petersen stage, or what was known as a mud wagon. It was pulled by four horses that many old timers classed as runaways.

open and the robber had gotten away with about $1,200 in gold bullion and $400 in silver.

It was believed that the holdup man took the loot to a small mill in Clear Creek where he and some accomplices milled the bars down into smaller amounts to avoid suspicion when it was shipped.

A newcomer to Old Kernville and a part-time miner and gambler, Jim Van Ripper, was blamed for the holdup, but nothing was proved against him. Later he was shot in a brawl and, with his death, the stage robbing era ended.

Early in the 1900's the automobile had moved from the realm of a luxurious toy and was being proven a practical working tool. It was the advent of the horseless carriage that caused Petersen to wonder if he really wanted to be in the stage business. His first mechanized stage was a Cadillac touring car he bought from John Swett. This was followed by a Stanley Steamer that blew up in Havilah three days after it was put into operation. Next came two Mitchells, one big and one small, which met with the same success as the others had. They wouldn't stop when the drivers hollered "whoa!" In other words, these drivers, even though they were at the top of their profession as reinsmen, and could not be beaten when it

113

came to handling stock, knew nothing whatsoever about mechanics. Moreover, there was no one to train them.

One thing after another happened until, in 1912, N. P. finally sold the stage line to Charlie Hand. In 1946 it passed on to Roy Orick, and from him to the present owners. Some of the old cars sat around the Petersen Ranch for years. The Cadillac was made into a pickup by Bill Cannon, who was handy with mechanical things.

N. P. Petersen was a trustee of the South Fork School for many years and, in 1902, was appointed to the Kern County Board of Supervisors to represent District 1. He was then elected to the Board in 1904, serving until 1909. During his term as Supervisor, the Hall of Records and the new high school (1906) in Kern County were constructed.

Say what you may for progress during the transition from horse and buggy to automobile, nevertheless a great deal was lost from the American way of life. Although it didn't happen overnight, the change gradually caused us to lose the closeness that was felt in those days for friends and neighbors.

In the early days a buggy might drive up in the yard any evening and, with a shout of greeting, all members of a family would come trailing in. As the team was put up in the barn for the night, parents would start catching up on the news as the kids ran off to play. There was always extra bedding and plenty of home-grown food. It created no problem if the visitors stayed a night or two. Sharing the same simple necessities brought people together. They shared more freely and seemed to be less critical of their neighbor's shortcomings. This, with a seemingly greater love for God and country, created a better place in which to live.

XVII Patterson Lane

WEST of the Petersen Ranch are the traces of the old short-cut road to Kernville. In the old days the first part of this lane, as far as the South Fork River, was called Patterson Lane. It was so named after J. M. Patterson, who settled on the west side of this old road. In 1870 H. L. Cook, for whom Cook's Peak to the southwest is named, also had a ranch along this stretch of road. Continuing north, past the old Petersen Ranch was the Lucien Barbeau place, later owned by Amos Petersen. The pioneer families of Woodberry Hay, John Simmon, and Stony Rhymes all lived here at various times, and their ranches along this stretch of road have since been covered by the waters of Lake Isabella. Just across the South Fork River was the James Fireball Ranch, later owned by Bob Stephens.

As the road turned west it passed the Carden Ranch. Bill and John Carden had first filed on this land and taken out water rights from the river. In the 1880's the Cardens sold out to John McCray, who in turn sold to his son-in-law, Cecil Hanning. A well-known landmark on this ranch is the rocky knoll that appears out in the field. In later years this knoll was known as Rattlesnake Knoll or Rabbit Island. It was on this ranch just in front of the knoll where the old South Fork School stood. Built in 1877 it remained there until it was moved to Weldon in 1921.

As the road continued on toward Lime Dike, it passed the Barrows place, later owned by Malloy, and purchased by Pete Brady. West of the Lime Dike came the Robinsons' homestead, and just before the old short-cut road

114

starts up and over the hill, it came to the Fugitt Ranch, later known as the Johnny Stine place.

Francis Fugitt, a Glennville freighter, married Eph Johnson's oldest daughter, Amanda, and filed on 160 acres just above the Johnson place. By 1891 he had sold this property to William Scodie and bought his ranch at the lower end of the Valley. By the time Frank and Amanda moved here they had six children — Edith, Thomas, Sara G. known as Lena, Harry F., William A. known as Dick, and Nelly May. The Fugitt children attended the South Fork School on the McCray Ranch.

On the ranch there were all types of wagons and buggies with stock to pull them, but the Fugitt children usually preferred to walk the two and a half miles to school. They would walk along the old road that went over the Lime Dike, picking up the Robinson and Brady children on the way.

Edith, the Fugitt's oldest child, set a record that has not been nor will it likely be surpassed. This was her teaching career that spanned 58 years. Edith started to grammar school in Glennville and after a time spent in the Weldon School, graduated from the South Fork School. Edith then made trips to the Bakersfield library by horse and buggy to check out books on algebra, geometry and related subjects.

Cecil Hanning, old-time cattleman of the South Fork.

She studied without benefit of a teacher, except the help she received from her aunt, Emma Johnson at the Weldon School. She then passed an examination for her high school diploma. Edith then completed a two-year course at the State Normal School in Los Angeles, later known as U.C.L.A., and received her general elementary teacher's credentials in 1894. Her first position was at the South Fork School where she taught all eight grades in the same wooden frame school house where she had spent so many childhood days.

Early in Edith's teaching career she married William Swett. This union was blessed by a daughter, Gertrude, who later became Mrs. Hess. Tragedy later struck, and Gertrude died giving birth to twin girls. These girls, who later became Mrs. Marlene Kroener and Mrs. Billie Smith, were raised by their grandmother without a break in her teaching.

Edith went on to teach in Kernville, Hot Springs Valley, Twin Oaks, and Old River before going to the Buena Vista School. There

South Fork School, built in 1877. *Left to right, back row,* Mr. Cheneworth, County Superintendent of Schools, Miss Bernice Bryant (teacher), Hester Palmer, Ruth James, Marguerite Palmer, Inez Leoneris, Annie Hanning, Hazel Cain; *front row, left to right,* Virginia Palmer, Thelma Petersen, Elsie Cain, Rolland Barbeau, Clyde Barbeau, Paul Leoneres, Garland Cain, Victor Gormez, Amos Petersen, Buz Palmer.

115

she served as principal for 25 years. When Mrs. Swett retired in 1956 she received meritorious service awards from the U. S. Senate and the California State Board of Education. She also received congratulatory messages from California School Superintendent Max Rafferty, Senator Walter Stiern and Governor Edmund Brown—quite an enviable record for this girl from the South Fork.

Another member of the Fugitt family who was well known on the South Fork was Dick, whose wife, the former Addie Petersen, was still living in Kernville in 1970.

Back of the Fugitt Ranch, along the river, was the Murphy Ranch. J. J. Murphy had first settled on this place, but soon sold it to Andy Brown and started clerking for him in his store at Kernville. All that can be seen of these pioneer ranches when the lake is down are the old ditches that were cut from the river. They too will soon be washed away.

Edith Swett and daughter, Gertrude.

XVIII Under the Waters of Lake Isabella

WHEN the lake was constructed a new section of highway had to be built. Starting one-half mile west of the Tradewinds Cafe, the road was swung slightly to the south as it skirted the last original ranch along the south shores of Lake Isabella. This was the Hillside Ranch, first settled in 1883 by John Beaty. The ranch headquarters were originally located at the south end of Patterson Lane but when the lake was formed they were moved farther up the slope. Soon after gaining title, Beaty sold to Andy Brown and became his ranch foreman.

As the highway gains the summit and starts down to Mt. Mesa, you can see the new headquarters of the Joughin Ranch. Before the lake was formed the ranch complex was north of the point of the hill. Reaching as far east as Patterson Lane, at one time it took in 800 acres, including the Patterson, Cook and Wes Brown ranches as well as the original Cannell Ranch.

Thomas Arthur Cannell was born on the Isle of Man in 1854. Coming to California with his brother, John J. Cannell in the 1870's, he joined him in the roving life of a sheepman. During a visit to his homeland in 1891 he married Margaret Ann Joughin, and they returned to California, settling almost immediately on the South Fork.

Mr. Cannell's brother-in-law, William D. Joughin, also came to the Valley in 1898, and after a year he started ranching in Inyo County with Bob Stephens, who was also from the Isle of Man. In 1907 Stephens and Joughin returned to the South Fork and leased the Cannell Ranch. Needing a crew of men to work the ranch, they immediately thought of a group of their friends from the homeland. The Isle of Man is small, only about the size of the South Fork Valley, and there wasn't much chance of advancement, so thirty dollars a month with board and room seemed a good offer. By 1909

Thomas Arthur Cannell.

William D. Joughin Sr., *on the right*, and an unidentified friend, in old Isabella.

quite a group were working on the ranch. These included William D. Kissack, Ed and Tom Kewin, Jim Kerruish, and Willie Kneil.

In 1912 William Joughin married Ethel Christian, daughter of Robert Christian, an early merchant of Kernville. They raised a son, William Jr., and after Mr. Joughin's death, young Bill continued to use the same family brand △ taken out by Cannell many years before and ran cattle on his Forest permit. The Joughins lost most of their farming land when Lake Isabella was formed, but they retained their summer permit for cattle in the high country, and still ran cattle on the lake bottom when the water was down.

In 1913 Kissack and Kerruish bought the old Batz place from Pat O'Brien, but in a couple of years Kerruish decided to branch out

on his own, and purchased the old H. B. True place. In 1914 William Kissack sent for his fiancee whom he hadn't seen for five years. Bill and Jessie Kissack made their home in a little cove against the hill.

All that was left of the old place in 1970 was a few of the trees that still stand, partly covered by the waters of Lake Isabella. In their home they raised two boys, William Jr. and Jim. In the 1930's the Kissacks acquired a permit in the high country, and in the 1940's expanded their holdings even further by buying the Bob Stephens place, thereby acquiring his cattle permit in the Sequoia National Forest.

These oldtimers from the Isle of Man worked hard and played hard. One of their favorite pastimes was racing horses, either saddle or

The Joughin Ranch above the lake.   **117**

The Kissack Ranch sets above the lake, and the fishermen try for bass around the trees that surrounded the old place.

Bill Sr. and Jessie Kissack.

buggy horses. You could always find one of them who was willing to stake his life on his claim that he had the fastest horse in the Valley. A group of the boys were coming home from the old town of Isabella one night when such a race took place. It was pitch dark and as they were going full tilt on a straight stretch just before the road came to the old Rankin Ranch, the race came to a sudden halt.

Some cattle had been lying on the side of the road, and upon hearing the approaching whirlwind a large bull decided he wanted to go to the other side of the road. He wandered right out in front of Mr. Kissack, which had almost the same effect as hitting a brick wall. The result was that Kissack spent considerable time in a Long Beach hospital with a broken collarbone.

When the land was purchased for the reservoir for Lake Isabella, the Kissacks moved up on high ground. More land was put under cultivation, being irrigated by well and sprinkling system instead of by ditch from the South Fork.

The last two ranches along the South Fork were best known as the Lower Rankin Ranch, just off the point of Kissack Cove, and the Luz Ranch. These lands are now submerged.

Much of the history of the South Fork will never be written as it lives in the memories of those who lived at the time, and in the minds of the succeeding generations who have listened to the stories told by the old folks.

Long, hard days spent in the saddle on the open range; dusty hours of back breaking work in the fields were the rule. Welcome breaks in the routine were provided by social activities enjoyed by the whole family. The Saturday night dance, the ice cream socials, the Methodist Church and the doings connected with it, were anticipated with much excitement.

There is something about the South Fork Valley that finds its way into the hearts of those who live there. Those who move away can never forget the time spent there, and often return. As the saying goes, "once you drink out of the river, you might leave, but you'll always come back."

Three South Fork Belles ready for a Sunday ride, 1913. *Left to right*, Hattie Smith, Helen Smith, and Ettie Powers.

Index

Kent, 41
Kerruish, Jim, 26, 117
Kewin, Ed, 51
Kiowa, 29
Kissack, Jessie, 55, 117
Kissack, Jim, 55, 117
Kissack, William Jr., 55, 117
Kissack, William Sr., 20, 55, 90, 117
Kissack, Mrs. William, 57
Kneal, Alphy, 111
Kroener, Marlene, 115

Labachotte, Pete, 13, 36, 37
Lacy, Mark, 36
Lagora, 4
Landers, John, 44
Landers, W. W., 10, 16, 20, 34, 44
Larson, Pete, 113
Laskey, Jesse L., 11, 12
Laskey, Bill, 12
Laury, Angela, 59
Laury, Joe, 59
Leazenby, Deak, 56
Lee, Mrs., 63
Leibel, Emma, 101
Leibel, George, 102
Leibel, Otto, 99, 101
Leoneris, Inez, 115
Leoneris, Paul, 115
Levey, Don, 12
Levey, Donald L., 12
Lightners, 9
Likely, Charles, 53
Livingston, Rev. J. C., 53
Loveall, Joe, 13
Lowell, Mabel, 17
Lowell, Joe, 113
Lowell, Sophie, 113
Luz, 118

Mace, 26
Mack, Gerald, 13
Mack, Henry L., 41
Mack, Jim, 44
Mack, Loren, 13
Malloy, 114
Martin, A. B., 60
McCay, A. D. C., 97, 101
McCay, Earl, 36, 106
McClure, Mae, 102
McCoy, Oliver, 30, 62
McCracken, 45

McCray, Clint, 35
McCray, John, 10, 16, 35, 114
McCray, May, 113
McDonald, Hoot, 29
McDonald, Margaret, 18
McDonald, Stanley, 18
McKinney, Jim, 45
McLaghlen, Andrew, 12
McLaghlen, Victor, 12
McQuirk, Pete, 102, 113
Mecham, Walt, 79
Mellon, Andrew, 12
Meriam, Ella P., 18, 52
Michel's, 20
Miles, John, 59
Miller, 16
Miller & Lux, 15
Miller, H. T., 95
Mills, M., 44
Milligan, Nellie, 55
Milligan, Harriet, 55
Milligan, Ray, 80
Miranda, 26
Miranda, Grace, 59
Miranda, Jesus, 16, 91
Miranda, Pete, 59
Miranda, Stephen, 92
Moreland, John, 102
Moreland, Mattie, 102
Moreno, Don Jose Saturino, 60
Morgan, 34
Morgan & Scott, 16
Mudd, Harvey, 12
Mudd, Henry, 12
Mulkey, Burel, 104, 108
Munchton, Clara, 95
Murphy, J. J., 20, 115

Neill, Bob, 54, 55
Neill, Dora, 104
Neill, John, 54
Neill, Miss Millie, 55, 108
Neill, Robert, 104
Newhall, Supervisor, 7
Nicoll, Alice, 49
Nicoll, Bill, 49, 62
Nicoll, Clara, 49, 55
Nicoll, Earl, 49, 59
Nicoll, Ed, 49, 59
Nicoll, John, 11, 16, 49, 59, 104
Nicoll, Mrs. John, 59
Nicoll, Willie, 35, 49, 81
Nilsson, Anna, 14

O'Brien, 16
O'Brien, Pat, 117
O'Brien, Patrick, 20
Olcese, 8
Oliver, Tex, 17
Orick, Roy, 113
O'Tea, Catilda, 59
O'Tea, John, 59
O'Tea, Mike, 59

Pablo, Tony, 23, 79
Packard, Jeff, 45
Palmer, Buzz, 63, 64, 96, 115
Palmer, Evelyn, 59, 96
Palmer, Hester, 96, 115
Palmer, Jim, 103
Palmer, Marguerite, 96, 115
Palmer, Robert, 63, 95
Palmer, Virginia, 59, 96, 115
Pascoe, Cecil, 12
Patterson, J. M., 114
Pete, Red Eye, 36
Petersen, 16
Petersen, Adeline, 109
Petersen, Amos, 110, 114, 115
Petersen, Howard, 109
Petersen, Lyman, 80
Petersen, N. P., 109
Petersen, Thelma, 115
Petersen, Walter, 109, 110
Petersen, William, 79
Pettypool, Charlotte, 52, 53
Pettypool, Ed, 16, 17, 53, 82
Pettypool, Gertrude, 16
Pettypool, Lottie, 16, 46
Pettypool, Nellie, 16
Phillips, Bernice, 6, 55
Phillips, Chuck, 6, 18, 55
Phillips, Earl, 6, 26, 27, 55
Phillips, Jessie, 6, 55
Phillips, Mike, 23
Phillips, Vic, 112
Pinon, John, 33
Polkinhorn, Jim, 103, 113
Potter, Eleanor, 55
Potter, Ruth, 55
Powers, Betty, 6
Powers, Bob, 78
Powers, Clara, 6, 19
Powers, Charley, 6, 7, 18, 36
Powers, Daisy, 6
Powers, Donald, 6
Powers, Druzilla, 7, 18
Powers, Eleanor, 18

Map of the South Fork

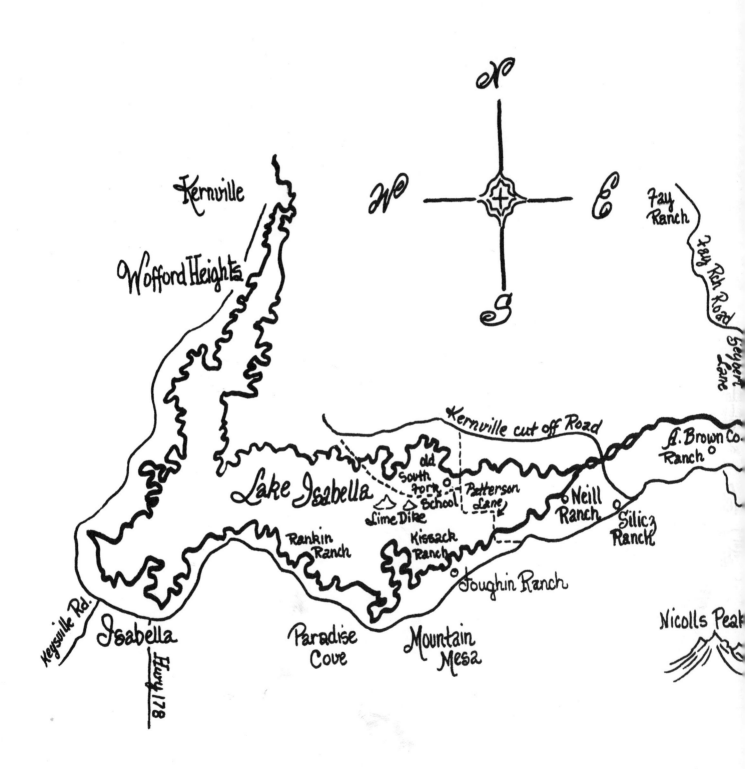

Kernville

Wofford Heights

Fay Ranch

Fay Rch Road

Seyert Lane

Kernville cut off Road

A. Brown Co. Ranch

old South Fork School

Patterson Lane

Lake Isabella

Lime Dike

Neill Ranch

Silica Ranch

Rankin Ranch

Kissack Ranch

Loughin Ranch

Keysville Rd.

Isabella

Hwy 178

Paradise Cove

Mountain Mesa

Nicolls Peak